The 13 Biggest Manifesting Mistakes and How to Fix Them!

*Stop Sabotaging Yourself
and Begin Loving Your Life!*

D1304474

By

Andy Dooley

Disclaimer: The author of this book does not dispense medical advice or prescribe the use of any technique as a form of treatment for physical, emotional, or medical problems without the advice of a physician, either directly or indirectly. The intent of the author is only to offer information of a general nature to help you in your quest for emotional and spiritual well-being. In the event you use any of the information in this book for yourself, the author assumes no responsibility for your actions.

For conscious creators who are ready to activate
their full potential and send positive ripples out into the Universe.
Can I get a namaste!

Linda,
I believe
in You!

Andy

2016

Linda!
I believe
in You!

Table of Contents

A Note From The Author

You're going to love this book!

No kidding! I am going to reveal to the 13 biggest manifesting mistakes, and if you're like me, I bet you're making at least 13 of them. Just kidding, maybe you're making at least half of them, daily. It's shocking I know! But don't worry, you're not alone.

These 13 almost invisible mistakes will murder your dreams!

How do I know about these mistakes? Because I have made all 13 of them thousands of times. But now, I'm much wiser.

I still catch myself making mistakes #1, #3 and #9. And #12. Okay, all of them. But now I catch myself and shift my vibration of attraction easily back onto the Bliss Train. My life has become so much better as a result of not making these mistakes repeatedly, and I want to help you to learn them so you can manifest all that you could ever imagine.

For the past five years, I have coached hundreds of clients. We've covered everything from wanting to manifest more money, desiring better health, attracting love and romance, going through divorce, starting a business, selling a business, and depression.

Again and again, I see the same errors showing up, and it doesn't matter whether my client is young or old, black or white, advanced or new to the Law of Attraction.

<u>We are all human and everyone, including me, makes these mistakes!</u>

That's why I wrote the book. It hurts me to see people like you making these devastating blunders, barely able to pay your bills and not coming near your full potential.

ENOUGH of sabotaging your success and happiness! Don't you think it's time you started living the life you have been dreaming about?

When I point these mistakes out to my clients and they start applying the tools and techniques I'm going to give you, positive change begins to happen and their lives open up the most amazing miracles.

For example, mistake #12 affects so many people from an early age of life. One of my clients finally broke free from it and manifested true love.

My clients have overcome depression, manifested large sums of money, new business clients, better jobs, weight loss and more.

However, it does take desire and conscious discipline to change these insidious habits. Are you finally ready to learn how to kick these habits to the curb? If you are,

The first step is: Identifying these mistakes.

The second step is: Admitting that you're making them

The third step is: Taking action and starting to apply the solutions.

Important Note: I cannot promise that after reading this book, you'll manifest the life of your dreams. I can promise that if you apply the solutions I share with you in this book, you will manifest positive CHANGE.

It's important that you are open and ready for change. And we all know that change can be unsettling at first! But change is good, always bringing an opportunity for something better.

Some of the changes may surprise you - some good and some (will appear to be) bad. Just know, in the long run, that it's all good!

Remember, you're on a spiritual journey and you will always be in the process of discovering more of your divinity and power to create a life you love.

This journey requires you to stay committed to becoming the best version of you, having fun and approaching life in fresh, new ways.

To get the most from this book, please set the intention that becoming aware of these mistakes and applying the solutions will be a turning point in your life.

Get excited about the possibilities of things changing for the best. All you need is one good idea, one new approach to handling an old problem. This book has 13 of them -- WooHoo!

Have FUN!

andy@andydooley.com

andydooley.com

4

I now know my divinity

I am clear and confident

I am a leader

I am guided by love

I am vibrating positive energy

I celebrate the contrast

I ROCK

I love my life

I am the creator

BIG MANIFESTING MISTAKE #1

I have a question for you: Are you tired of struggling to figure out this manifesting thing? Are you wishing it would just hurry up and work?

I mean, you can manifest the little things all day long - spare change for a latte, a parking spot right out front, a free cupcake - but when it comes to the big stuff, the stuff that really counts like the relationship, getting out of debt, new clients for your business, a new job, good health, it feels like it's taking forever!

Don't despair! You are in the right place! And I am really excited you are here because, just like you, I wrestled with this manifesting thing for years before I finally figured it out. Yep, that's right. Andy Dooley, creator of Vibration Activation ™ and co-founder of TUT.COM, went through years of struggling before finally figuring out how it all works.

Today I'm going to share with you the #1 biggest manifesting mistake that I can almost guarantee you're making if you're not getting consistently stellar results. This mistake is strangling your ability to create a truly awesome life!!!

I had to learn about these mistakes the hard way, so now, if you pay attention and take action on what I'm saying, you don't have to go through all the heartache and struggle I did.

I want to compliment you in advance for reading this book. I know you're a lifelong learner, and you know that what got you here (this level of mastery of life) is not going to be what you NEED to get you there (the next level.)

So read carefully and thoroughly, because if you apply what you're going to learn in this book, it can create a big shift for YOU!

If you're like me (and I know I am like me), you are into spiritual stuff and you have studied and worked to apply the

Law of Attraction. And it's possible you have manifested some really big things in your life - a new job, clients in your business or maybe you met and fell in love with that special someone (but now they drive you crazy). Maybe you even lost some weight or won a cruise to Mexico.

You were on fire! You had this LOA thing down!! But then it stopped working, and the next 12 or 18 months sucked. What's up with that!?

It's strange, but I see it happen all the time. When you're NOT trying to manifest…awesome things are just falling into your lap. But when you get serious and try to create the money to get out of debt or attract your soul mate and lose the weight, it backfires and you end up gaining weight, attracting weirdoes and accumulating more credit card debt.

Don't you hate that?

I know I did! I used to have a mountain of credit card debt, and I owed the Internal Revenue Service. But I turned it all around! And you can too.

For too many people, the Law of Attraction is the law of NO satisfaction! And I don't want you to be one of them!! And neither do you - that's why you're reading this book, right?!

For millions of people, manifesting what they want - what they REALLY want - is A <u>COMPLETE MYSTERY.</u>

There can be no mastery when it's a mystery!

Wouldn't you agree? Well, I am going to help you shift that.

Okay, so what is this BIG manifesting mistake that I see YOU making and that I used to make all the time, too?

Before I tell you about this EPIC, colossal mistake that is slamming your dreams to the ground and holding them for ransom, let me share a quick story....

In 2007, I was in the worst place of my life. I was broke financially. I was also in physical pain, as my lower back felt like it had a samurai sword stuck in it. And I had a broken heart. Yep, I fell in love - she was THE ONE - and then, it was over. It was the worst. I put myself to bed and had a pity party.

Have you ever thrown yourself a pity party?

Of course, my situation was not my fault! I could not have manifested this into my life! I needed someone to blame. I blamed my mother, then my brother. Then I got honest, looked within myself and you know whose fault this was... Deepak Chopra.

All joking aside, I had to take full responsibility for my pathetic situation. I created this and I will fix this.

Now today, I know that everything that's happening in my life is my creation - 100%. There are no accidents or mistakes in my life or yours. Everything is unfolding in divine order. Everybody is exactly where they should be according to their thoughts, beliefs and expectations. But back then, I was looking for a reason that my life was such a mess.

I was lying in bed - in HEARTBREAK HELL - with one question running through my head, and I'm sure it's the same question that you have asked yourself when all hell broke loose in your life:

How did this happen to me?

Have you ever asked yourself that question? How did this happen to me? How?

Why? Who's to blame for it all???

I mean, like me, you've read all the books on positive thinking. Like me, you've attended the seminars and meditated for hours. And yes, I have a beautiful vision board. You should see it - me and Jennifer Aniston in a Ferrari!

How - since I was "doing all the LOA stuff" - did THIS happen to me?

Here's how: I had <u>Lazy Lousy Focus.</u> THAT was a BIG mistake I was making, and I was not even aware of it!

And listen up: If you are manifesting more of what you DON'T want than what you DO want, my friend, you are in the grips of <u>Lazy Lousy Focus</u> just like I was!

For weeks before I ended up on the floor with a samurai sword in my lower back, I was focused on all the mistakes I'd made in my life.

The key word there is **focused.** I was focused on my mistakes, feeling bad and stupid for making them, and focused on "why" it all happened the way it did.

You see, because I was heart-broken, and FOCUSING on all my failures, I was stuck in a negative vibration. I kept attracting more of what I did NOT want.

I was having the world's biggest pity party ev-ah!! Maybe you can relate?

The LOA dictates that what I am FEELING is what I am attracting. True or false?

Because you are a student of LOA, you know that what you focus on creates what you feel and how you feeeeeel is how you attract.

Now here's something you might not realize about LOA. When you have yourself a pity party, like I did - I call this the

Bitch Train, and I'd bought myself a first class ticket - not only does it attract "negative" experiences, but it also feeds itself with your own subconscious thoughts and memories.

So guess what happened to me?

Because I was focused on my failures, the LOA went on a mission to find every bit of supportive "evidence" from my life that said, "Andy, you're an idiot, and your dreams are never going to come true." Man, I was a real mess! Riding the Bitch Train is not fun.

LAZY LOUSY FOCUS SYNDROME, which is how we end up on the Bitch Train, can be super frustrating - until you figure out how to shift.

It's pretty simple once you realize it, but when you're in it, and you're heart-broken, staring at a mountain of debt or with the

IRS knocking, you just can't "see" how your focus could be anywhere else but on the problems. OR maybe you don't even know what you're focusing on. It's really perplexing.

BUT, my friend, I am going to tell you: Your focus has to be on what you WANT - not on what you DON'T want - or you will never get out.

In every moment, you have a choice to focus on the positive or negative! I got out, and I'm going to tell you how right now. Ready? Great!

So Lazy Lousy Focus Syndrome is like a virus that starts when you forget that you create your own REALITY! You're letting REALITY - what's "out there" - kick your ass!

You have to remember you are the creator of your experience.

When you believe that reality is something that is happening to you, you become a victim of the reality that you actually created. CRAZY. It's like a hamster wheel with spikes!! OUCH! Around and around you go, and it just keeps getting worse and worse! It's terrible, I know, but we all make this mistake.

The question is: Why? Because your ego says that you'll "solve" the problem that way, by paying attention to what's wrong. But no, no, no - THAT IS the problem. You've got to FOCUS on what you want so you start attracting it to you!!

So here's what I do to shift my vibration of attraction when I find myself riding the Bitch Train. It's quick and easy, and I've been practicing and teaching this for years:

I say: **"Stop. Cancel. Clear. Get the fear out of here!"**

See how easy that is!! Now, for some of you, at first it's going to require saying it like a dozen times every hour on the hour. But with time it will get easier and less frequent.

Over the years that I've been teaching Vibration Activation™ and working with hundreds of clients from all kinds of backgrounds, I have discovered that people often think their problem is something different from what it really is.

My clients will come to me and say they have a money problem or a weight loss problem. That's the problem they THINK they have, but the money, the weight or the no-relationship is just a symptom. It's not the cause. Let me say that again. It's a symptom! And that's true for all of us.

The cause of the problem is LAZY LOUSY FOCUS. You keep focusing on what you don't want. Then you talk about what you don't want, and then you tell the STORY about how hard it is and you can't figure it out. "I've tried everything, and nothing works for me." Sound familiar?

When you find yourself going on and on about what you don't want - riding the Bitch Train - well you gotta just STOP. CANCEL. CLEAR! GET THE FEAR OUT OF HERE! You're operating out of fear instead of LOVE.

When I was having my pity party, I kept FOCUSING on what I did not want, and the LOA kept giving me more.

You can't say "I don't want that, I don't want that," over and over because you're giving what you don't want your energy and FOCUS, so it's then active in your vibration and you get more of what you don't want!

It's all about STOP. CANCEL. CLEAR. GET THE FEAR OUT OF HERE.

Then once you stop, cancel and clear the fear, you have to change your focus. HOW? By asking yourself questions. And these questions will help to change your focus.

ASK yourself this: **"What is good in my life right now? What is working?"**

If you ask and truly want to receive, you will be given answers that will make you feel good, and that will shift your FOCUS and vibration of attraction.

FOR EXAMPLE: Maybe you start focusing on how you're always struggling with money. You're not good with money, and everything is so expensive. "I never seem to have enough money. It's not fair. There's just not enough."

STOP. CANCEL. CLEAR.

GET THE FEAR OUT OF HERE!

Then ask yourself the question:

"What is good in my life right now? What is working?"

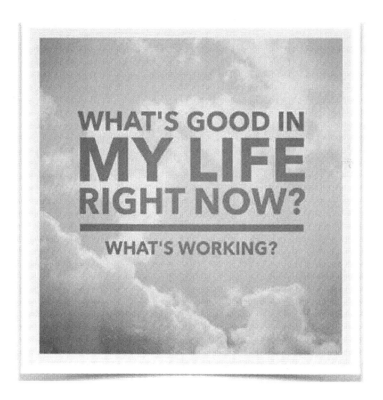

This will shift your focus onto the positive in your life. Now, I know it did not solve your money problem, but it very successfully stopped you from riding the Bitch Train about money. It stopped you from focusing on your lack and limitation.

I am curious. What *is* working in your life? Although I possibly don't know you personally, I do know this: You're breathing. You have a roof over your head. You're smart enough to be reading this book and taking action. Every day, you're getting closer to the life you want. The Universe loves you, and you're being guided!

It's simple, although it's NOT EASY, because LAZY LOUSY FOCUS is a habit like smoking. You can break it, but it will take diligence and commitment. No one can do it for you, but I have faith in YOU! I believe in you!

To get the most out of this book, be sure to read and take action on all 13 mistakes. The benefits will be awesome in your life :-)

QUICK REVIEW: Starting today, when you find yourself on the negative train of thought, a/k/a the Bitch Train:

Say "STOP. CANCEL. CLEAR. GET THE FEAR OUT OF HERE!" BONUS: Another version would be, **Stop! Cancel! Clear! I will not live in fear!**

Then ask yourself this questions to change your focus:

"What is good in my life right now? What is working?"

FOCUS on what's going well! This will instantly shift your vibration, and you'll start attracting good things into your life.

Okay, that's the first big manifesting mistake and its solution. Applying the "Stop. Cancel. Clear. Get the FEAR out of here" is a lifelong process because we live in a reality of positive and negative. Have fun stopping the Bitch Train and shifting your focus! You can do it!

Let's move onto the second big mistake that is killing your dreams.

BIG MANIFESTING MISTAKE #2

Every day, you and I experience a thing called PROBLEMS! They are everywhere. As soon as you solve one problem, another problem shows up! It's impossible to get rid of problems - they're like fleas.

Nobody wants problems. We all want a problem-free LIFE! Or do we?

I USE a different word for problems. I use "CONTRAST." Shifting from seeing problems as problems to understanding problems as contrast will help you fix Big Manifesting Mistake Number 2.

Thanks to Abraham-Hicks for shining a spotlight on the word "contrast" and making it part of the Law of Attraction vocabulary.

Once I started seeing my own problems as CONTRAST, everything shifted for me. I learned how to SURF the waves of CONTRAST, and I am going to teach you how right now.

You see, that which is a problem for one person is an opportunity for another. It's like the old saying, "One man's junk is another man's treasure." It's all about perspective.

The word "problem" does not feel good. But the word "contrast" has no judgment about the situation. It is not good or bad, it is just... CONTRAST.

What exactly is CONTRAST?

When I was a professional actor going on auditions for theater, I was told to bring a headshot and two contrasting monologues. That meant one monologue would be light and fun while the other was more dramatic.

The difference between these two monologues was CONTRAST!

The difference between you wanting to be wealthy and having credit card debt is contrast. The difference between you being really excited about life and feeling depressed is CONTRAST!

That's all it is! It's not GOOD or BAD! It just is what it is!

BIG Manifesting Mistake Number 2 that I see everyone making is not embracing the gift of contrast. Instead, they see CONTRAST as a curse, a problem. And then they spend more time focusing on the problem.

You're about to learn how CONTRAST is your best friend and how to receive the gifts it always brings.

Once you look for and see the gifts of CONTRAST, your life will get so much better.

Most of us think that once we become enlightened, our problems will disappear and rainbows and unicorns will follow us around everywhere we go. WRONG! We never escape contrast. If, every time contrast shows up, you think something is wrong with you, then you're going to beat yourself up and create resistance that prevents you from manifesting your desires.

If you remember from mistake #1, I failed at achieving my dreams. I had a mountain of credit card debt and was broken-hearted. I was having a pity party. This is a perfect example of CONTRAST!!!

Because of this massive CONTRAST, I became super CLEAR on what I wanted my life to be like. But let me tell you, it was hard to get out of the negative downward spiral, because I kept focusing on my failures and what I did wrong. So I used the "STOP. CANCEL. CLEAR. Get the FEAR out of here!" because I was suffering from Lazy Lousy Focus Syndrome.

I was not seeing the GIFT of CONTRAST!!!

Instead it was the CURSE of CONTRAST

My vision of how I wanted my life to look did not match up with my reality. Has that ever happened to you? Of course it has.

Congratulations! CONTRAST has just given you a gift.

You see, from contrast come two very important gifts.

Number one is CLARITY! Ah yes, clarity. Clarity is power. When you get really clear on what you want, the whole Universe can start working to bring it to you!

But until you're clear and focused, you second-guess yourself. You keep asking other people's opinions. You're stuck in limbo. Remember that out of contrast comes clarity.

The second gift from contrast is...DESIRE! Desire is the elixir of life! Desire is what propels us forward as individuals and as human beings!! DESIRE is GOOD! Within every desire is strong attraction power.

Out of contrast, desire is born!

When I was broken-hearted, a new desire was born within me to fall in love again and manifest an even better relationship! When I was financially broke and owed the IRS, my desire to make big money was stronger than ever.

Every desire you have summons creative energy to you. Do you realize that without contrast, your life would be boring? You would not have any desires. You would not grow, contribute and become more.

So stop using the word "problem" and start using the word "contrast!" And don't try to get rid of contrast. Do you realize the only people without CONTRAST are DEAD!!!! Life is in the living, YO!!! Say it with me: "I LOVE CONTRAST!!!" Say "I LOVE MY LIFE! I am the creator, and I ROCK!"

Remember, every time you experience contrast, it gives you two gifts:

CLARITY and DESIRE.

Now I want to give you two questions to ask yourself every time you experience contrast. This way you can extract the two gifts.

1. **"What do I want instead of this?"** This question brings you clarity!

For example, you go to a restaurant and receive slow, rude service. Boom! That's not a problem, that's contrast! What do most people do in this situation? Bitch and complain. But then they're more focused on the problem then the solution. *Get it???*

So you experience bad service, which is contrast. Now you ask the question, "What do I want instead of this?" BINGO! "I want good service. I want a polite server that greets me with a smile and is upbeat. I want a kitchen that has plenty of cooks/servers who are ready to go. I want my food to taste great and be served in a timely manner."

Do you see how contrast gives you clarity and desire, and when you focus on what you want, you shift the energy and what you're attracting to you? (I love this stuff!)

2. **What is the feeling behind the desire?** Ask yourself, "What is the feeling I want?" Then find a way to start feeling it ASAP!

For our restaurant example, the feeling behind the desire was to be served in a positive, timely manner and to feel respected and valued. Simple. Then put ALL of your FOCUS on what you want and start feeling it now!

By asking these two questions, CONTRAST becomes your best friend, therefore correcting Manifesting Mistake Number 2.

Here's a metaphor that you'll find helpful. Imagine that we are all surfers on the ocean of life. There is no land. It's just you, the ocean and your surfboard. Sometimes the waves of life become big and rough, and at other times they are fun and easy.

You see, when the ocean is semi-calm, it's easy to paddle around and get to where you want to go. But when the wind starts blowing, it creates waves - waves of contrast - and you can either surf the waves or let the waves beat you up.

The better you are at surfing all types of waves of contrast, the more fun you can have on the ocean of life. But if you see all waves of contrast as problems, then your life is going to be very hard.

I highly recommend starting today. See all your problems as waves of contrast and surf them, dude!!!

When you learn to embrace all contrast, then you will become a playful, powerful creator.

Here's a quick review: You don't have problems. You have contrast, and you will never get rid of contrast! The next time you experience contrast, ask yourself two key questions.

1. "What do I want instead of this?" This question brings you clarity!

2. "What is the feeling behind my desire?" Start feeling it ASAP.

If you are going to LIVE the LIFE of your DREAMS, then you must start looking at CONTRAST as your new best friend! CONTRAST GIVES YOU CLARITY, and clarity is power!!! From contrast, new desires are born, and that gives you the FOCUS and FUEL to align your vibration with your desires, making manifesting easier.

I promise your life will never be the same once you know and live this truth that CONTRAST is your best friend. Say it with me, "I CELEBRATE the CONTRAST! Contrast is my best friend!"

BIG MANIFESTING MISTAKE #3

This third mistake is huge, and there is NOT one person I have met or coached who is NOT making this mistake! Everyone makes it, including me. It's a pandemic, a dream killer.

This is a recurring mistake that even the masters make. But it won't affect you anymore, because by the end of this section, you will have a simple, powerful tool for being able to stop making this BIG mistake.

Are you with me?

Quick review: You probably remember from mistake #1 that back in 2007, I was broke, physically and financially, and I was spiritually confused. Life basically sucked.

BUT I learned several crucial new habits when I made the decision to exchange my sucky life for the amazing one I have now. (Did I tell you how much I LOVE MY LIFE??!! I do - I REALLY do. My life is amazing now.

You see, I am LIVING the life of my dreams. I am helping people transform their lives. I am traveling the world doing workshops, coaching clients, speaking, writing, making videos.

I am debt-free, and I am making six figures a year! WOW! I LOVE MY LIFE!

And I am about to share with you one of the most important things I learned when I made the decision to have this awesome, amazing, fun and fantastic life.

SO WHAT MADE THE DIFFERENCE?

I'll tell you what made the difference. When the cops finally came and busted up my pity party, I recommitted myself to studying metaphysics and the LOA.

During this time, I invested thousands of dollars in workshops, coaches, audio programs, books and online seminars. I went through year after frustrating year of trying to figure out a manifesting process that could produce consistent results. I was determined to figure it out and solve the mystery!!

I remember listening to an audio program in my car by Craig Valentine. He said, "What got you *here* won't get you *there*." Craig was the Toastmasters' World Champion of Public Speaking in the year 1999, and when he returned home after winning the world championship, he went right out and bought another book on the art of public speaking.

Craig had heard a quote from Will Rogers that went like this:

"Even if you're on the right track, you'll get run over if you just sit there!"

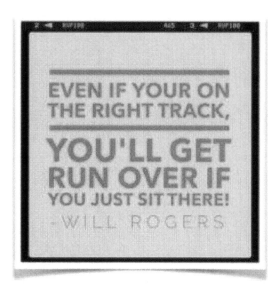

Have you ever been on the right track and just sat there? Or worse, YOU got run over? That's why it's so important to commit to following through and taking action with everything you're learning in this book.

Inspiration such as that from Craig Valentine made a difference for me. How was I able to turn my life around? I recommitted myself to being a student and learning everything I could about Law of Attraction and metaphysics. I was on my own personal quest to find a process that works consistently.

And - no surprise really - I couldn't find it in one neat little program, so I gathered exactly what worked and put it into my own "neat little program" called Vibration Activation™! I'm so thankful for this process that works 100% of the time when I put it to work. These manifesting mistakes are an integral part of my Vibration Activation™ process.

AND they are a great place to start! Are you ready to discover mistake #3?

It will change your life forever, and I know that's a big promise.

Before I tell you what it is, let me set the stage for why it's such a big deal.

Looking into your past, have things you wanted to manifest taken longer than you thought they should? Longer than you wanted them to? Be honest: Are you STILL waiting for them to show up?

The point I want to make is simple. Your desires are almost always going to take you longer than you THINK!

So what does this mean?

It means you suck at manifesting. NO, I'm kidding! You don't suck at it, but you do need a major tune up...dare I say...a major ACTIVATION of your vibration.

It means you must start factoring "old man time" into your

manifesting equation. While your desire is available INSTANTLY as a vibrational reality, physical manifestation has to work through the dimension we call time. That's why it can seem like it takes longer to "show up" than you want.

This is not being negative or pessimistic. It's working with the laws - all of them!

So BY DESIGN and because of the LAW, most of the time your "big desires" are going to take you longer than wanted, which is called LAG TIME. You can use this to your advantage!!!

If all your desires manifested instantly, you and I would be in BIG TROUBLE!!!!

LAG TIME helps you get FOCUSED and clear on what you really want. It helps you figure out the why behind your desires.

There is always going to be where you are and where you want to be. And all of your creative power will always be right NOW. That means all of your power will always be in the MEANTIME. Your life is lived in the MEANTIME! True or TRUE?

Are you following me? Are you getting this?

BIG mistake #3 is... You're Not Enjoying The Meantime!

THIS IS a DREAM KILLER! WHY? If you're annoyed and frustrated about the LAG TIME, then every day you're creating more resistance around your desires, and you're riding the Bitch Train again.

Remember, the Universe does not deliver any of your desires to the Bitch Train. It can only give you more of what you don't want when you're on that train.

Here's the solution for fixing mistake #3. I want you to write this down and remember it.

If you DON'T enjoy the meantime, it will be a LONG TIME!

If you enjoy the meantime, it will be a short time.

This is HUGE and vitally important to your success and happiness. If you do not enjoy the MEANTIME, your desires will be a long time in manifesting. And YOU have already experienced this, true or false?

But if you enjoy the meantime, it will be a short time. Did you get that?

If you enjoy the meantime, it will be a SHORT TIME!!!!! WHY? HOW does this work?

If you don't enjoy the mean time,
IT WILL BE A LONG TIME!
If you enjoy the meantime,
IT WILL BE A SHORT TIME.

How you feel is how you attract. And if, in the meantime, you're frustrated and annoyed that it's taking too long, then you, my friend, have resistance. Resistance is a vibe killer and slows everything way down. What is resistance you ask? Resistance is what happens when you let your day to day focus on what's wrong with your life dominant your life. Focusing on what's wrong makes you feel awful. That awful feeling lets you know you have resistance and it means you are not allowing your abundance to flow.

When I was stressing out about how am I going to pay my mortgage, will I have to sell my house? The more I beat myself up and focused on how hard life was and how stupid I am, the more resistance I created within my vibration of attraction. The Universe was trying to bring me opportunities to help me get out of debt. But because my lazy, lousy focus was on the negative I was not able to attract the opportunities to make more money. But then I got wise to the resistance I was creating, I used the Stop. Cancel. Clear. All my power is here. I asked better questions to change my focus and got clear on what I wanted. I embraced the contrast and took positive action. By doing this I released my resistance and money making opportunities started to show up.

Are you guilty of wanting things to happen right now? WE all want overnight delivery.

It's so simple to eliminate this resistance. ENJOY THE MEANTIME, and it will be a short time!

I LOVE it, and it WORKS! One of the most important things I did to turn my life around when I was broke and lost was to begin enjoying the meantime! My clients who have turned their lives around have all gotten really good at enjoying the meantime.

This means you have to be conscious every day of how you're really feeling. If you find you spend eight or ten hours a day frustrated and annoyed with other people or yourself, you've got resistance.

Pay attention, as this is really important. You must stop sugar coating how you really feel with affirmations you say but don't believe. Affirmations that are lies can NOT work!

You have to take responsibility for how you really feel. Start by accepting where you are in your life right now. ACCEPT your bank account, accept your body weight and accept your relationship status. Once you own it and accept it, you can change it. YES!

Here's one of my favorite Andy Dooley quotes:

"Your situation can't get any better until you feel better about your situation."

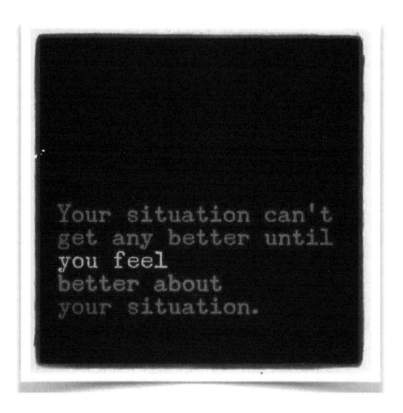

Question: Are you ready to start FEELING better about your situation? I am sure you are, but if you're dependent on your situation changing first and then you'll feel better...DANGER, DANGER!

You have to change your thoughts, your attitude and your perspective about your situation. That will change how you feel, and then your situation will start to change. You must CHANGE FIRST on the inside before the outside will change.

Find as many ways as you can right now to ENJOY the meantime and your desire will be a short time.

It happens every week. One or two of my clients will find themselves fighting their reality, forgetting that they are the ones who have indeed created their reality! I know what that's like. I sometimes get caught up in REALITY and fight it! But every time we fight with reality we lose, because reality is past tense. It's old news! Reality is left-over pizza.

The reality you're living today was created from the thought vibrations of last month! That is why it's vital to look away from REALITY and create the feeling and vision of yourself being, doing and having the life you want to live. Give thanks for exactly how your life is now and celebrate it! ENJOY THE MEANTIME!

Here are two practical things you can do right now that will help you enjoy the meantime:

1. Make friends with everything and everybody in your life. Stop fighting and resisting change and wanting other people to be different. Make the best of every situation. Pause and do this every day, three times a day!!!!

Years ago when I was at my lowest point in life, every hour on the hour, for months on end, I had to make the best of my situation and enjoy the meantime. **It's your golden ticket.**

2. The best vibration you can send out to the Universe is one that says, "I like or appreciate where I am," which is enjoying the MEANTIME. Also, be excited about what's coming, even if you're unsure about the future.

The best is yet to come.

That's the sweet spot, and you have been there before. You do know what that feels like. My full audio program, "Vibration Activation," will get you vibrating there consistently.

The solution to mastering mistake #3 is, starting today, YOU MUST ENJOY THE MEANTIME and your desires will be a short time! This is not just a one-time thing. Enjoying the MEANTIME is for the rest of your life. You can DO IT!

Okay, here's a quick review of all 3 Big Manifesting Mistakes!

Mistake #1 involves suffering from lazy and lousy focus. The solution is to start saying, "STOP. CANCEL. CLEAR. GET THE FEAR OUT Of HERE!" Ask the question, "What is working in my life?" and focus on the positive because how you feel is how you attract. BONUS: Another version would be, Stop. Cancel. Clear. I will not live in fear! Or Stop. Cancel. Clear. All my love/power is here!

Mistake #2 is learning how to embrace the gift of contrast. You must start surfing the waves of contrast. Know that contrast is your best friend. Out of contrast comes clarity and desire. Ask yourself, "What do I want? What feeling am I after?"

Mistake #3 is you're not enjoy the meantime. Then it will be a short time. I know this might sound simple, but it's the simple things in life that often have the biggest impact.

Holy dancing unicorns and rainbows! WOW! You'll want to review these first three mistakes again and, more important, start applying the action steps! It takes consistent action and repetition of the basics to become a manifesting rock star and create what you REALLY want in your life.

BIG MANIFESTING MISTAKE #4

The EGO wants to know HOW it is going to happen and when it will happen. Your EGO is the Horrible HOW Monster.

Do you realize the EGO is always trying to prove itself right? Your EGO is the part of you that often lives in fear and has forgotten who you really are. Once your fearful self creates a belief, it will protect itself and always try to save face.

So many dreams never get off the ground because the EGO can't figure out HOW it's going to happen.

Then it creates a story about HOW it can NOT happen to prove itself right and protect you from looking like a failure. Meanwhile, your Inner Spirit Guide has access to Infinite Intelligence and can easily connect the dots and guide you with positive emotion to the next step.

When you have a desire, your conscious mind starts figuring out HOW to make it happen - who you need to call, where you need to go, how much money it will take, etc. Your ego, operating from fear, forgets that you are a divine, sublime, cosmic, conscious creator. It overlooks the fact that you have access to Infinite Intelligence and that you have an Inner Spirit Guide you can call upon to lead you.

Remember, your EGO is the part of you that often operates out of fear. It's okay to think logically about HOW it might happen and take logical steps forward that feel good, moving you in the direction you want to go. But be aware of over-thinking the HOWS! That's when the HORRIBLE HOW MONSTER will take over and create a bogus story of HOW it can NOT happen!

The easy way to do it is to LET GO of the HOW and stay focused on the WOW! The WOW is the feeling!!! You are always after the feeling!

Don't burden your conscious mind over-thinking HOW it is going to happen!!!!

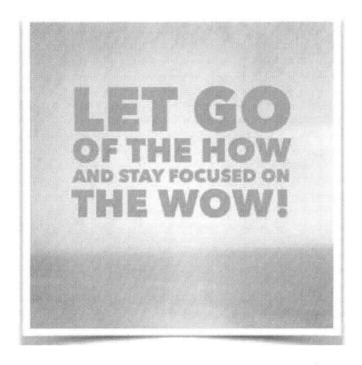

Although most people want to KNOW HOW, all you need to know is what is before you NOW!

It's not your JOB to figure out all of the HOWS. Your part is to decide what you want, focus on it, FEEL IT, give thanks and take one step at a time toward it! SIMPLE as that!

Often times I'll hear a client say, "There's this thing I really WANT, but I don't have it yet!"

This is splitting your focus and stops your desire from coming to you.

Because of your split focus you're actually vibrating the LACK of your desire, which is very different from vibrating the feeling AS IF you already had your desire!

When you get stuck trying to figure out the HOW of your desire, you are actually sending out a vibration that is not a vibrational match to your desire. You are working against the Universe! The Universe is trying to deliver your goodies, but it can't find you because your vibration is one of lack! You're on the wrong channel, dude!

Here's an example from the world of weight loss that you will likely understand.

A common desire for millions of people is to lose weight! So of course you think you need to think of HOW you will lose weight! What action steps are you going to take? Will you change your diet, buy a treadmill, join a gym, start running or will you simply starve yourself? These are all logical things you would do to lose weight, but these are all the horrible HOWS.

FURTHER, these approaches have been created from a place of no pain, no gain, from a place of taking action to make it happen rather then find the feeling first.

These plans come from a place of "We are mere mortals of flesh, bone and blood." What about who we really are? As divine, sublime, cosmic, conscious creators, we are made of vibrating energy, and when we change our inner vibration, we can easily change our body.

When YOU change your core vibration, YOU can easily change your body image.

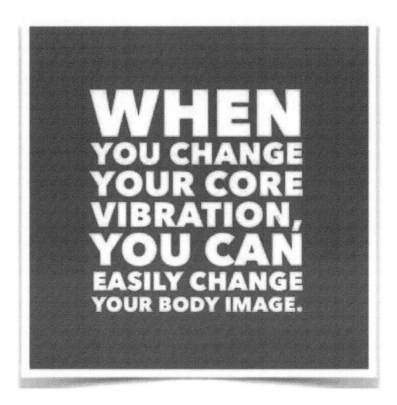

The previously - mentioned action steps of no pain, no gain are taken from a place of lack, from a place of thinking, "I am not there yet. I am still overweight."

Here's the way to let go of the horrible how's and take the right action steps toward weight loss.

- **FIRST: Redefine your desire.** What you really want is to feel good and look great.

    - You want to eat foods that give you energy.

    - You want to make peace with your food.

    - You want to enjoy eating.

    - You want to feel good and healthy.

    - You want to eat to live, not live to eat.

    - You want to be excited about your life.

    - You don't want to worry about food.

You want to feel good so you can be there for your kids or partner! You want to have lots of energy. You want to be the best you can be.

You want to love your life! That's what you really want - to love your life!

To love yourself!

Can you feel the difference in that compared to the desire, "I want to lose weight because I am fat and I don't like myself?"

So what you really want is to:

- Love yourself

- Love your life

- Be excited about life

NOW you've got clarity on what you want and what it feels like.

SECOND: Start feeling like you are already that person. <u>Start feeling confident, strong and energized. Start feeling healthy and slim.</u> Yes, start feeling slim and trim! You might need to close your eyes, but you can imagine how it would be to feel slim!

FEEL GOOD about where you are and where you're going. Be the person who does not make food a big deal. Be someone who eats only what they believe is good for them. Be someone who looks great and values their health and respects their body!

THIRD: NOW that you're starting to feel like that person, take action, do the things you feel that person would do. FEEL your way into taking action - that is HOW you do it! That is HOW you line up your vibration and move forward with action steps that are in alignment with your true desires. That is HOW you stay in alignment with your desire.

Taking action is an important part of the process, but it's taking action that feels good and is in vibrational alignment with your real desire that will produce amazing results for you!

REVIEW

Step 1. Redefine your desire by getting clear on what you really want!!!

Step 2. Start feeling like that person, and start being that person! Start living there!

Step 3. Take action from that good-feeling place. Go ahead and think about the logical steps of how you will get there, but make sure those HOW TO steps are from a place of excitement and enthusiasm!!! This way, you're working with the Universe instead of against the Universe!

HERE'S AN EXAMPLE from my life: I wanted to become a professional speaker and life coach! I decided that HOW I was going to get there would be through the Toastmasters organization! Every year, they have a big international speech contest and designate a world champion of public speaking. I thought that if I won this contest, it would be easy to become a professional speaker and life coach! It made perfect sense.

So I took action and became a member of Toastmasters. I joined two clubs and entered into the speech contest four years in a row!!! Much to my surprise and shock, I never became the world champion of public speaking!

OH NO!!! My big dream got flushed down the toilet!

HERE was my mistake! I was focused on HOW I was going to become a professional speaker and life coach!

Toastmasters was an invaluable experience for effective communication and leadership skills, but after NOT winning for the fourth year, I let go of the HOW and simply refocused on becoming a professional speaker and life coach! BUT HOW was I going to get there? What steps did I need to take?

Step 1. I got clear about what I really wanted and the feeling I was really after, which was to become an expert on the Law of Attraction and a life coach. I wanted to make a difference in the world and transform people's lives by showing them the fun and easy way to apply the LOA in their lives.

Step 2. I started being that person - I started acting the part. I spoke everywhere I could, and most of the time, it was for free. I started to walk my talk and be who I wanted to be.

Step 3. I took inspired action after communication with my Inner Spirit Guide. I operated from the place of <u>"I am who I want to be."</u>

What actions was I inspired to take? I started doing one-man shows at Orlando Fringe Festival. (I did three, in fact.) I took acting classes and did lots of improv comedy. I continued going to Toastmasters and was inspired to start teaching a workshop on speaking and comedy geared toward Toastmasters. It was scary at first because I had never done that before, **but it soon felt right and I was very successful doing that for**

over two years. I had no idea where that would lead, but it continued to feel right. I kept taking inspired action, and the HOW-to steps just showed up! One thing led to another, and speaking and coaching opportunities started coming in. Fast forward... today I travel the world as a Law of Attraction expert, professional speaker and Vibration Activation™ coach - doing what I love! I also created the Vibe Tribe.

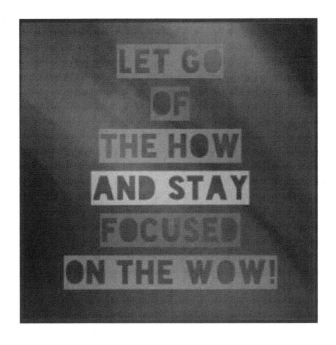

I am thrilled to say it worked out even better then I imagined. I love Toastmasters and what I gave and gained from my experience there, but I am happy I did not become the world champion of public speaking, because now I am the world champion of Vibration Activation™, and the world is my oyster!

I let go of the HOW and stayed focused

on the WOW!

The EGO (the Horrible How Monster) has very limited knowledge compared to your Inner Spirit Guide, who has full access to Infinite Intelligence.

It's a thousand times easier if you focus on the solution, the feeling of THE ANSWER! You know my favorite quote: "Feeling first, manifestation second." It applies to manifesting creative ideas and finding answers, too!

Let your Inner Spirit Guide give you the inspiration of HOW to get there. You stay focused on the feeling, which puts you into the receiving mode of the answers and HOW TO steps. Then take action - get up and go!

My book *iManifest* goes into more detail on how to take inspired action and understand your Inner Spirit Guide! (The book is available on my website.)

Okay, so mistake number 4 is trying TO FIGURE OUT THE HOWS OF MANIFESTING! Let your Inner Spirit Guide figure out the HOW. Your part is to be happy and stay focused on the WOW, which is the feeling! WHEN you are feeling good, you put yourself into the receiving mode so you can hear the HOW-TO STEPS from your Inner Spirit Guide!! Then take action!

Remember that when you ask, it is always given! FEEL the success and happiness NOW! That way, you'll keep the communication lines open between you and your Inner Spirit Guide, and you will be able to prevent the Horrible HOW Monster from eating your dreams!

Many people really struggle with the HORRIBLE HOWS of manifesting, and I want to make sure I give you my best info! Thanks for reading and also remember the solutions I am giving here are not the end-all. PLEASE combine what I am giving you with what is already working for you. Be an alchemist of transformation as you explore and try different things. Mix and match and maybe create something new. AWESOME, DUDE! U totally ROCK!

BIG MANIFESTING MISTAKE #5

This next mistake is super big, and if you get it wrong you will experience much PAIN, FEAR and even DEPRESSION.

Start applying what I'm about to give you, and you'll experience lots of JOY, LOVE and LAUGHTER!

First, let's simplify emotions. There are really only two emotions: There is love, and there is fear. All of the positive emotions come from love, and all the negative emotions come from fear.

Many people believe that they are at the mercy of their emotions. It seems that their emotions are something that just happens to them, and they often feel attacked. I agree that is exactly how it feels. I have been there myself and know what it's like to feel depressed, rejected, stupid, angry, frustrated, overwhelmed, scared and befuddled. I also know love and joy, goofy and silly, wacky, wild and funny. Outrageous and totally titanium, dude! I have surfed all the emotions! That's right, dude!

Where do they come from? Emotions come from the bottom of the ocean. Just kidding! Emotions come from within you and are a form of communication from your Inner Spirit Guide. (By the way, I call that voice within your Inner Spirit Guide, but some people refer to it as your Higher Self, angels, God Force, Inner Being, etc.)

You are never alone. Your Inner Spirit Guide is with you all the time and has access to Infinite Intelligence. Your Inner Spirit Guide is Source Energy, and you are an extension of Source Energy in the physical form. (Thanks, Abraham-Hicks!) Every emotion you have ever felt or will ever feel is your Inner Spirit Guide communicating with you. Let me say that again:

Every emotion you have ever felt or will ever feel is your Inner Spirit Guide communicating to you.

If this is the first time you're hearing this, you may have your doubts. I totally understand, and I'm not trying to force this on you. Just be open-minded and try it on for size to see if it makes sense.

This next section is done in a Q & A format.

Where do emotions come from? Again, they come from your Inner Spirit Guide. Your Inner Spirit Guide, who loves and adores you, who worships the ground you walk on, is aware of your every thought, word and desire. It is communicating to you or is giving you guidance (however you want to look at it) in the form of emotion to help you reach your desires. Sweet emotion.

Why do we have to feel emotions? We feel the emotions from the inside because when we have an undeniable gut feeling about something, it's hard to ignore it. That's the way it's supposed to be, because if it was another form of communication, it could get lost in the translation. Unfortunately, many emotions that we feel have gotten lost in translation because well-meaning doctors, philosophers, psychologists and other people with fancy letters after their names have misinterpreted the meaning of emotions and have also tried to profit from them. A common solution in today's society of negative emotion is to take a pill, which does NOT deal with the underlying problem. People also try to deal with negative emotions by drinking alcohol, smoking, over-eating, and shopping.

When we try to soothe our emotions with food, drugs, or alcohol, we only make the problem worse. And you know what the problem is every single time??? (It's so stupid, it's stupid!)

Every time you feel negative emotion, it means one thing and one thing only. It means that you're forgetting that:

Heaven is on earth and everyone is an angel.

It means you're forgetting that life is an illusion, and we are all actors on the stage of life! **The painful emotions you** experience are gifts that are meant to bring you back into alignment with your divinity!

When you feel negative emotion, you can always trace back the emotion to a thought you are thinking or a belief that you hold that is out of alignment with who you really are. It's out of alignment with "heaven is on earth and everyone is an angel."

Let me ask you a question: Do you actually believe that heaven is on earth and everyone is an angel? I think if you're reading this book, you have likely done enough spiritual study and meditating to arrive at a place where you see that heaven and hell are both on earth - it just depends on each person and how they focus and how they interpret what they see. And of course, you can see how human beings can easily be seen as angels or demons. That's the beauty of living on Planet Earth in a time-space reality where we have **free will** to see the good in other people or see the bad. Thanks to the Law of Attraction, what we focus on will feel good or evil to us, and what we feel, we will attract!!!

Therefore, heaven and hell are on earth. For each individual, their current mental focus and their thoughts and beliefs about life in general determine what they feel and experience. :-)))

We all have different experiences, but we all experience the same emotions. What if somebody says something to you and it comes off the wrong way? Suddenly you're angry or feeling hurt/betrayed. On the surface, it appears they made you feel it, but underneath the surface, it's only you who determines how you feel!

NO one can ever make you feel anything without your permission! It's you that is thinking the thoughts and holding the beliefs that trigger the emotional response. EMOTIONS do not attack us. We evoke the emotions! We feel certain emotions because of the thoughts we think and the beliefs we hold. Simple as that!

Now, if you're suffering from any type of chronic illness, I agree with you that it FEELS like your emotions are attacking you, and who knows when you'll suddenly feel completely depressed, tired or angry? But WHY do you feel attacked!? It's because of the underlying beliefs YOU hold about yourself, other people and life in general.

You are holding beliefs that are not in alignment with your Inner Spirit Guide, who always sees that heaven is on earth and everyone is an angel! ANY time you see things differently, you're going to experience negative emotion!

Did you hear that!!! Let me say that again!!!!

You are holding beliefs that are not in alignment with your Inner Spirit Guide, who always sees that heaven is on earth and everyone is an angel! ANY time you see things differently, you're going to experience negative emotion! Isn't that an awesome explanation? I love it!

Here's a question that comes up often: HOW do we get control of our emotions!!?? We do that by understanding that emotions come from thoughts and beliefs about ourselves and life in general. All emotions can be traced back to a thought we're thinking in the moment or a belief we're holding about life. The way most people deal with negative emotion is to numb it in order to ignore it. As mentioned above, they go to their physical body because that's where they feel the negative emotion, and they eat chocolate or other food, smoke a cigarette, and drink wine - anything to numb the pain. That is so stupid!! ALL you have to do is CHANGE the thought or belief! So simple!!!! So simple!!!! It's an emotional joke.

For example, you might feel negative emotion because someone you love is not being very loving back to you. Maybe you feel ignored or rejected. The underlying (and lying) belief could possibly be, "I am not important, I don't matter, or I am not good enough!" WELL, that is a LIE!!! You are inherently good enough, and you are important! Just because they're not being very loving toward you doesn't mean they don't love you anymore. Their behavior is violating one of your beliefs that says something like "If you really love me, you would give me your full attention all the time. You're not doing that when I need you, so I am choosing to feel hurt, ignored and unloved."

It's you who is forgetting who they really are and who you really are. You are angels of love and heaven is on earth. When you stop the nonsense, you remember that the love you're trying to get from the outside is already inside of you and that the other person is an angel.

It's not their job to love you - it's your job. It's you holding the belief that "I am NOT good enough or I am not important" that makes you feel like you have to get LOVE from someone else instead of realizing the truth: YOU ARE LOVE and YOU ARE MORE THAN ENOUGH! Oh sweet relief. Can I get a Namaste!

Here's another common question:

Will I always feel negative emotions? Yes! There will always be contrast, and you will temporarily get caught up in the illusion and find yourself riding the Bitch Train. Then you'll say, "STOP. CANCEL. CLEAR. Get the fear out of here!" You'll then be able to shift yourself out of the illusion of fear, get off the Bitch Train and get back onto the Bliss Train, feeling good!

Here's yet another common question: **How do I go from feeling angry, overwhelmed or depressed to happiness?**

First, don't try to make a quantum leap! Be okay with feeling the negative emotions, knowing it's not who you are but just what you're feeling in the moment! You're not that wave of emotion. You are the ocean of love and joy. That is who you are at your core.

Second, CHANGE the thought that is causing the negative emotion!!! Or change the belief! HOW do you do that? Ask yourself this question: "What is it I am thinking about (fill in the blank) that makes me feel (fill in the blank)?" **In our previous example,** if you get upset because someone you love is not behaving in the way you think they should, you might feel the negative emotion of anger. Then you ask yourself the question, "WHAT AM I THINKING about this person that makes me angry?" INSTANTLY you will be presented with answers to what you're thinking or believing that is causing the negative emotion. It works every time!!!! You're probably thinking that they should know better or "Why are they not doing it my way?"

Whatever the situation, when you ask the question and really want the answer, you will be given that answer, and then you can examine the thought or belief in the light of love. Remember, your Inner Spirit Guide will never ever agree with you that this person is wrong or bad.

Your Inner Spirit Guide will always see this person as an ANGEL and heaven as being on earth!

SUMMARY: Let's wrap up our new understanding of emotions. ALL emotion is communication from your Inner Spirit Guide to you! Negative emotion means you're forgetting that heaven is on earth and everyone is an angel, including yourself. Positive emotion means that you're moving in the right direction to manifest your desires. You're fully connected to Source Energy, and you're flowing that positive energy!!!

Okay, so mistake #5 is failing to understand your emotions! From this day forward, you will always KNOW that there are only two basic emotions, LOVE and FEAR, and when you forget who you are, you will feel negative emotion. When you remember who you are, think positive thoughts and see the best in yourself and others, you will experience positive emotions. Don't you love how simple it is?!!!

SOLUTION: Here are 2 Simple Steps!

1. When you feel any negative emotion ask yourself the question, "What is it that I am thinking about (fill in the blank) that makes me feel (fill in the blank)?" Immediately you will be given answers. Then examine those answers and ask yourself "Is it really true? Or is it just my perception?" Another bonus question to ask is this: "In order for me to feel this emotion, what would I have to believe?" You will again be given an answer. Then ask yourself, "Is that who I really am, is that who they really are, is that what is really going on?"

2. Remember, we are all actors on the stage of life. Life is a dream world of illusion. Your Inner Spirit Guide is always

going to see the world as "heaven is on earth and everyone is an angel," including you! When you forget this, you will experience negative emotion! Remember that you are never, ever the negative emotion. It is just a wave of emotion passing through. You are the ocean - the ocean of love and joy!!

Once you master your emotions, which is easier than you have been led to believe, you will start living happily ever after! Emotions are everything, because they are how you feel, and we all want to feel good! This leads me into the next biggest manifesting mistake....

BIG MANIFESTING MISTAKE #6

Sometimes the most important things in life are not so obvious!!!

True or false? TRUE! You think feeling good would be really IMPORTANT and obvious! You think it would be on the top of your to-do list! But most people have it backwards. They think that if they can just manifest the new house, dream job or relationship, then they'll at last be happy!

Have you ever found yourself intently pursuing a desire so that once you achieved it, you could be happy? Confess! I know I have! I am guilty!

This is called the "IF - THEN" formula, which equals a life of needless suffering.

It goes like this:

"**If** I get my degree, **then** I can be happy!"

"**If** I make a lot of money, **then** I can be happy!"

"**If** I lose 20 pounds, **then** I'll feel better about myself, start dating and do something with my life!"

Have you ever played this game with yourself? Are you playing this game right now?

Okay, we MUST turn the "IF - THEN" formula around. Flip it so it reads:

"**IF** I AM HAPPY, **THEN** I can lose 20 pounds."

"**IF** I start feeling good, **THEN** I can manifest more of my desires!!!"

You know my favorite Andy Dooley quote: "**Feeling First, Manifestation Second.**" You have to feel it first before the manifestation can take place!!

Now let's talk about WHY feeling good is so important. I think you know, but let's dig a little deeper into the world of vibrating energy!

Simply PUT, how you feel is HOW you attract!!! How you feel in the moment is determined by what you are focused on and what you're thinking. How you feel is also made up of your beliefs and expectations!!! All of this creates your vibration of attraction, and the good old Law of Attraction brings you everything that is a vibrational match to the vibration you're sending forth to the Universe. Woohoo!

That's why feeling good is VITAL to your success and happiness.

The mistake many people make is creating a bunch of **rules** about what has to happen in order for them to feel good, such as "I have to make a certain amount of money to feel good" or "I have to fall in love with my soul mate and then I'll be happy!" You see how easily we can fall into the IF - THEN trap?

That is why it is so important to enjoy or feel good about the journey - to enjoy the process, enjoy the unfolding of your desire. Recently, I was talking with a VIP client of mine who was telling me they have finally arrived at the place of really enjoying the unfolding of desires, of having fun watching all the pieces come together!

Another way to understand how important it is to feel good is to think of yourself standing at the doorway to your kingdom. The KEY that opens the door is… feeling good! Feeling good is not knocking on the door. FEELING GOOD opens the door to your kingdom! That might be challenging for some of you to believe if you are new to metaphysics and Law of Attraction! BUT I promise you that FEELING good is everything in this world of vibrating energy in which we live!

Yes, everything is vibrating energy, and you are ALWAYS getting or manifesting what you match up with vibrationally. How you are feeling is the vibration you are sending out, and the LOA is responding to your vibration!

Therefore, HOW you feel IS how you attract!!! **FEELING GOOD IS EVERYTHING!** From this day forward, your NEW #1 priority is to FEEL GOOD NO MATTER WHAT!!!!

What happens if you're not feeling good? DO NOT TRY to jump to feeling GREAT! That's like trying to jump from the Bitch Train headed south to the Bliss Train headed north.

Just find a thought that will improve how you feel right now in this moment, such as "This will not last forever. Everything always works out for me." Ask a question: "What is working in my life? What can I appreciate right now?"

These questions will shift your focus! QUESTIONS do that! Questions are powerful!!! Then focus on something that feels good, and in a matter of seconds you'll start feeling better!

For example, right now I want you to think about and focus on someone who is easy to love!!! If you want to think of your dog or cat, then think about them. Right now focus on the love you have for them. Visualize their happy face.... Now I bet you're feeling better! See how easy it is? BOOYAH!

Now the trick is to shift how you feel when you're not feeling good, such as if you're depressed and sitting in front of the TV all day, focusing on everything that is wrong and what you don't like or want!!!

You should not have any more excuses!!! Ever! There is NO excuse for not feeling good... NONE! There are so many amazing things you can focus on and think about that will make you feel good! The world is filled with beautiful, joyful experiences. Your life is filled with happy memories! Use them to change how you feel. Don't let reality kick your ass. Remember, you create your REALITY!

Another one of my favorite Andy Dooley quotes is this:

REALITY IS MY BITCH! Please don't allow yourself to be offended by the use of the word "bitch." I am using it strategically to wake you up from the trance that we put ourselves in every day. We forget this very important piece of information about creating our own reality, and we let the reality we are focusing on or complaining about make us FEEL BAD. NO, NO, NO, never again! Reality is your creation, so don't get upset about the reality you've created. Let it go. FORGET about it. It's yesterday's news.

TAKE back control of your life by making feeling good your #1 priority!!!! WHY? Because how you feel is how you attract!!!

Now here's the other Andy Dooley quote I love so much and I mentioned it earlier! This is the **MOST important** part of FEELING GOOD!!!! You know what it is by now, right?

"FEELING FIRST, MANIFESTATION SECOND!"

This is VITAL to your success and happiness. YOU MUST, MUST feel good first, and then you'll experience the manifestation second!

But don't make yourself FEEL GOOD to hurry up and manifest your desires. That's like saying affirmations but not really feeling or believing them. FEEL good simply because it feels GOOD! THAT'S WHY you want to feel good - NOT to hurry up and manifest your desires.

FEEL GOOD NOW! Or feel the best you can now! And if you have been depressed, then the best feeling up from depression is anger, so get angry! Then from anger feel revengeful. Then from there, go to annoyed, to frustrated, to hopeful, to positive, to optimistic, to happy! YAY! It's like climbing a ladder out of the hole!!! I wrote more about that in my book <u>iManifest.</u>

OKAY, so mistake #6 IS NOT KNOWING HOW IMPORTANT IT IS TO FEEL GOOD! THIS SOUNDS LIKE A NO BRAINER, BUT I AM SURE YOU AGREE THAT MOST PEOPLE HAVE NO BRAIN! OR AT LEAST THEY FORGET TO USE IT.

SUMMARY: FEELING GOOD IS EVERYTHING because how you feel is how you attract! You want to FEEL GOOD right now NOT so you can manifest your desires but because feeling good feels good! Don't demand that other people behave differently so you can feel good. Feel good now because then you can shift your focus and ASK better questions. ALL your power is NOW!!! Can you feel it? Go ahead right now and feel good that you're reading this book. Feel good that you know this info and you're alive to experience it and share it with others.

Go ahead! I double dog dare you to feel good right now! Go ahead and put a big silly grin on your face! SMILE. DO IT for you, not me. Do it to prove to yourself how easy it is to FEEL GOOD at any time. DO it for no other reason than to FEEL good right now!!!! Woo hoo! See how easy it is to feel good?

Do you realize the moment you feel good. You're attracting everything good into your life.

Here are 2 Simple Steps to activate your positive mojo:

1. Become a FEEL GOOD ARTIST! This means that no matter where you are, no matter what is going on around you, you can always find a way to feel good! How do you do this? By directing your focus, by deliberately focusing on what is working and what is GOOD! By looking for the positive in every situation!! Then magnify it and FOCUS on it until you FEEL IT, until you have shifted your vibration of attraction. If you become a FEEL GOOD ARTIST, your life will take off!

2. Remember, REALITY IS YOUR CREATION! Don't let reality slap you around and then put you on the Bitch Train! Stop playing the "IF - THEN GAME!" "If I lose weight, then I'll be happy." FLIP it to read, "If I am happy, then I can lose the weight! If I am happy, which means if I feel good, then I can attract my desires!" See how simple it is to start living happily ever after!? It's all about feeling good NOW! And

NOW you KNOW HOW! Woohoo! Boom-Chic-A-Boom!

So far, I have shared with you six mistakes and their solutions. There's a lot of great content here, and I want to make sure you get the most out of your investment.

Before we move onto big mistake #7, let me ask you some questions.

- So far what ah-ha moments have you had?

- What solutions are you excited about applying to your life?

- When are you going to apply them?

- Where are you going to apply them?

- How are you going to apply them?

Take a moment to answer these questions. Now visualize yourself doing it and SMILE!

Great ideas and solutions to problems are worthless without action.

Okay, let's review and digest the last 3 Big Mistakes.

Number 4 was OVER-THINKING HOW IT IS GOING TO HAPPEN! Never mind how it's going to happen. Focus on the feeling as if it has already happened! Think less and visualize more.

Number 5 was UNDERSTANDING HOW YOUR EMOTIONS ARE THE KEY TO MANIFESTING. When you're feeling negative emotion, ask the question: "What is it that I am thinking about (fill in the blank) that makes me feel (fill in the blank)?" Immediately you will receive answers. Then examine those answers and ask yourself "Is it really true? Or is it just my perception?" Another bonus question to ask is this: "In order for me to feel this emotion, what would I have to believe?"

Your Inner Spirit Guide is always going to see the world as heaven is on earth and everyone is an angel.

Number 6, which we just covered, was: knowing how important it is to feel good! You must become a feel good artist. Then, no matter what is happening around you, you can always feel good! This, in turn, makes you attract all your goodies with less effort and more fun!

Now it's time to move unto the seventh biggest manifesting mistake which is....

BIG MANIFESTING MISTAKE #7

Lucky #7 is all about LOVE.

Let me ask you a question. Do you want to meet your soul mate and fall in love? Of course you do. Here's how. LOOK in the mirror, mate, and say hello to your soul.

A big mistake I see so many people making, myself included, is...looking for love in all the wrong places.

Why do so many of us make this mistake? It's because we're looking outside ourselves.

The LOVE we really want is inside us.

LOVE is a huge subject to cover, so I am going to get right to the core of it. We all want to be in love with that special someone and have a romantic relationship. We get brain-washed at a young age into believing that there is one person out there, our knight in shining armor or our princess, who is going to make us happy and cause us to feel loved for the rest of our life! We start out young on a quest to find true love that will last a lifetime, and many of us end up broken- hearted and even scared of love and life! OUCH!

The fairytales and movies rarely portray the main character STOPPING on the quest for love and learning to love themselves first. One of the most famous movies of the 1990s was *Jerry Maguire*. At the end of the movie, Tom Cruise decides that Renee Zellweger is the one he loves and busts into the women's group, giving a romantic monologue to win her heart. She responds with the famous line, "You had me at hello!" Both characters were looking for love in someone else. They didn't love themselves completely, so they wanted to find someone who would fill that gap.

In *Jerry Maguire*, Tom Cruise says, "You complete me!" Awwwww.

Everyone eats that up, but if you're looking for someone to

complete you, that's like dying of hunger and trying to fill up on sugar candy.

Now I know that you KNOW better, and of course you're not looking for someone to COMPLETE YOU! You know it's your job to LOVE yourself. BUT look at the relationship you're in now. How's it working out for you? Be honest with yourself. Can you say that you really do love yourself and you are giving your love easily and freely?

What if right now you are single? Do you really want to be single? How long have you been single? Why are you single?

I bet you have a good story about why you're single. For years I was single, but as of writing this, I have met a very special woman.

During my single years, I learned to appreciate and love myself more than before. I've had some amazing relationships along the way that taught me much about myself and love. It has been a beautiful journey. I know as long as I am loving and appreciating myself first and not looking for someone to complete me or make me happy, I will always be attracting amazing people into my life, cultivating great connections along the way. So in the meantime, I am enjoying life, doing what I love to do and feeling excited to watch my current relationship unfold.

Whether you're in a relationship now or single, the real question is: **Do you love yourself?** Can you look in the mirror and love the person you see? If you can, congrats! That's awesome. If you can't, don't worry, because I am going to give you some simple tools that will help you fall in love with YOU.

How do you learn to love yourself? Start by liking or appreciating yourself or life in general. Start simple. I remember hearing Abraham once recommend taking self, meaning yourself, out of the equation. STOP trying so hard to love yourself. Just start appreciating everything you can in your day-to-day life. Appreciate your living conditions, appreciate your friends, appreciate music, and appreciate your life on a deeper level than before!

APPRECIATION is a very powerful vibration. I believe it's better than LOVE. Yes you heard me right! WHY? Because the word LOVE means so many different things to everyone, and for many people, LOVE is a four-letter word.

Here's a quote from Abraham about the vibration of appreciation:

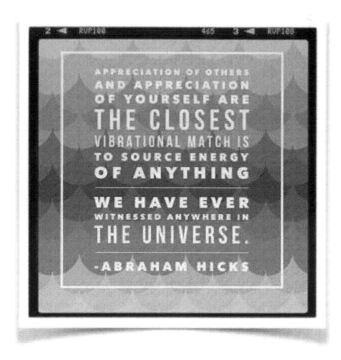

"Appreciation of others and the appreciation of yourself are the closest vibrational matches to Source Energy of anything we have ever witnessed anywhere in the Universe."

So your vibration around the word LOVE is out of whack. It's not a pure vibration, but the word and vibration of APPRECIATION are not all messed up with fairytales. People are not saying to one another, "I appreciate you so much that I would die for you!" No one has ever said that. Or how about this in a story book, "They fell deeply into appreciation and lived happily ever after?" No one says that!

Tell me, have you not done some stupid things in the name of love? I know I have! And what did it get you? A broken heart, possibly an expensive divorce, and years of frustration because you thought you knew what LOVE was. That's why singer/songwriter Waylon Jennings wrote the song, **"LOOKING FOR LOVE IN ALL THE WRONG PLACES!"**

Now don't get me wrong. I am not criticizing the word "love" or saying LOVE is a bad thing. I know some of you reading this book are in a beautiful relationship, and every day you feel so much LOVE for yourself and your partner. Congrats! I am happy for you. But the rest of us are getting beat up by this word!

THAT is why I am highly recommending the word APPRECIATION, which can easily lead you to LOVE - but a LOVE that won't leave you bitter and heart-broken.

By taking the word "SELF" out of the equation, you can

instantly find so many things in your life to start appreciating. That's what you want to do - start feeling the emotion of appreciation more and more! Then you're buzzing with appreciation and feeling good. And we know all about the importance of feeling good! Right? (Wink, wink!)

WHY IS LOVING YOURSELF SO IMPORTANT?

It's because how you FEEL about yourself creates a dominant vibration within that you send out to the Universe! Each one of us has a vibration about money, food, diets, politics, relationships, and the list goes on. Each of those topics creates a vibration of attraction for you!

BUT how you feel about yourself trumps all of those vibrations because you take you everywhere you go. SOOOOO, not liking and loving yourself can really mess up your overall vibration.

LET'S do a simple exercise NOW to get you feeling LOVE and APPRECIATION:

Right now, think of someone who is easy to LOVE. To make this even easier, think of a child, a grandchild or a beloved pet....

Since dogs and cats are usually the easiest, feel free to think of your most loved pet. Go ahead and feel the love you have for them. Imagine you're shining a spotlight on them. Visualize their happy face.... Say their name the way you call them.... Feel the love.... Do you have a cute nickname for your pet? Say the nickname now.... Do you feel yourself filling up with LOVE? Sweet LOVE! Feel it more, see their face, feel their love....

Now direct that LOVE toward yourself! Yes, turn that spotlight of LOVE onto you. Feel your own love. Give yourself all your LOVE.

NOW that is what it feels like to LOVE yourself! Guess what? You can do this anytime you want. Any time of the day, you can flood yourself with love sweet love!

Okay, so mistake #7 is not loving yourself and looking for love in all the wrong places. The only place you will ever find true everlasting love is within yourself. Can I get a Namaste!

Now let me give you two ways to ADD LOVE and appreciation to your life!

ONE: Change the conversation you're having in your head. First notice how you're talking to yourself, notice the tone of voice. Do you know when you are the most loving? It's usually when you're talking to your pet! Right? You ooze love and appreciation for your pet, as experienced in the previous exercise. You talk to them in the sweetest, most caring voice EVER!

What would happen if you started using that voice on yourself? (They would lock you up!) What if you started silently speaking to yourself with a nurturing and encouraging tone of voice? Remember that thoughts are powerful. The more positive thoughts you speak to yourself, the more you're going to create a positive vibration within yourself.

TWO: How do you treat yourself? Do you work crazy hours? Do you starve yourself, then stuff your face with food, then go to the gym and punish your body? Do you sit on the couch and feel sorry for yourself?

Most people put having fun at the bottom of the list! We actually put ourselves last. We take care of everyone else first, and then there's no time for us. We burn ourselves out! I know I am guilty of this one. I have gotten so much better, but it's still a work in progress. All of these actions say we are not taking care of ourselves. Actions speak louder than words!

Then some people finally reward themselves with a bottle of wine, drink the whole darn thing, and wake up hung over and hating themselves. STOP THE MADNESS! And start the kindness and appreciation for yourself!

HERE ARE SOME SIMPLE THINGS YOU CAN DO to activate a vibration of self-appreciation!!

Indulge yourself. Yes, get a weekly massage, go to the movies, be NICE to yourself, compliment yourself, go to your favorite restaurant, take a class and learn something new or take a hot bubble bath.

Ask yourself what is something simple you could do that would light you up easily and shift you into a positive vibration?

For the LOVE of appreciation and yourself, DO IT EVERY day and/or week! Right now write something down that you will do every day or week to activate the vibration of self-appreciation!

When you take care of yourself, the Universe will respond and take care of you! It's the LAW! BUYEAH!

Here's the SUMMARY:

If you want to feel love every day, you must start appreciating LIFE! Make it the highest priority to start appreciating everything every day! Make no excuses. Our time on planet earth is going by so fast. Start appreciating everything NOW.

Over time, this deeper level of appreciation will turn into SELF-appreciation! Then self-actualization!!! Call it self-love if you want. :-) Regardless of what you call it, you will be feeling Source Energy flowing through you, and you will be happy and living with passion! You will have arrived at Nirvana.

BIG MANIFESTING MISTAKE #8

It's unanimous!!! It's across the board! Everyone including YOU feels like you should be further along in your life! How do I know this? From years of coaching and doing workshops and from my own personal life, I've seen it again and again!

For example: You thought by now you would have lost that final ten or 20 pounds. You thought by now you'd be rich and famous. You thought by now you would have written that best-selling book and be on top of the world! You thought by now you would be happily married - or joyfully divorced but you're still married to THEM!!! Surprise, surprise, surprise!

Everyone feels that they should be further along! Let me say this again: *Everyone feels that they should be further along!*

This feeling causes RESISTANCE, because you are comparing where you are to where you want to be. Don't do that - it's a vibe killer!

You see, out of contrast, desire and clarity are born and you're inspired to take action. That's a beautiful thing! It's working! Isn't contrast great? Remember, contrast is your best friend and reality is your creation.

But because your REALITY is so in-your-face every day, you are constantly reminded of where you are in relation to where you want to be! There's a tug of war going on that creates the resistance! As soon as you ACCEPT where you are and make peace, then the TUG of WAR is over. Your resistance subsides, your vibration raises and the things you desire can start finding their way into your life.

That means right now you have to be okay with your body weight and your relationship or lack of relationship. You have to be okay with your credit card debt, your disease, your bunions, your crappy job and stupid boss. You have to enjoy the Meantime, as mentioned in mistake #3.

Now when people first hear this, they say "BUT if I make peace with where I am and accept my situation, the Universe will think I am happy where I am and not give me my desires." WRONG!

Accepting where you are and making the best of it is NOT giving up on your desires! It's letting go of the resistance that keeps your desires from coming to you! Here's one of my favorite Andy Dooley quotes. LOL!

Your situation can't get any better until you feel better about your situation. (I know I said this earlier, but it's really important!)

WHY is this? Because how you feel is how you attract. YOU have to change your thoughts, beliefs and attitude about your situation so you can start feeling better, and then your situation can change.

A great example of letting go of resistance is when a couple is trying to start a family! They are doing everything they can to get pregnant, but it's just not happening. This starts to create resistance. Then they get to a point where they have tried everything and finally surrender AND accept their situation.

They make peace with not being able to have kids or they decide to adopt and then...she gets pregnant! This does not always happen, but it's very common!

It happened with my sister, who was trying for over a year. Nothing happened, and then she and her husband adopted a beautiful little girl, Calli. A few years later, my sister got pregnant with Sarah. Now I am the crazy uncle!

How often have you experienced letting go and then it happens? Maybe you wanted a job or certain position, you finally gave up on it, and then some time later the job/position fell into your lap. Or maybe you tried every dating website, singles club and speed dating to no avail. You finally gave up, but what you really did was let go of the resistance of trying so hard. You finally made peace with your situation, and then that special someone walked into your life!

If what you want has not happened yet, then it means one simple thing: You are not in alignment with your desire, meaning you have too much resistance around your desire. They go hand-in-hand, and it's a simple FIX!!!!

Right now, ACCEPT where you are and make the BEST of it! If your current situation really sucks right now, I know that accepting it is not what you want to hear! You have a strong desire to take action and FIX it now!

Unfortunately, most people who try to fix it, fix the wrong thing!!!

THEY try to fix the outer world! WRONG!

Trying to fix the outer world is like looking in the mirror and trying to give yourself a smile by putting your fingers on the mirror to lift up the corners of your mouth. NO, NO, NO, you would not do that! If you looked in the mirror and wanted to see a smile in the reflection, you would first smile on the inside!!! Then the smile would show up on your face and be reflected back to you!

You have to FIX the inner world, which is your vibration!!!! Your vibration is made up of your thoughts, beliefs and expectations.

Does that make sense? I know you have already been trying to FIX IT the old-fashioned way. How's that working out for you?

If it's not working out for you, that's why you're reading this!

That's why you have to ACCEPT where you are and let go of all of that resistance!!!

A great affirmation I created that you can use when you are feeling annoyed about where you are is to say:

"I am where I am, it is what it is, plop, plop, fizz-fizz, oh what a relief it is!!!"

"I am where I am" is very powerful because you are accepting where you are in life. You have to remember that the BLISS Train will take you where you want to go! It knows what you want but can't get you there because you have the brakes on!

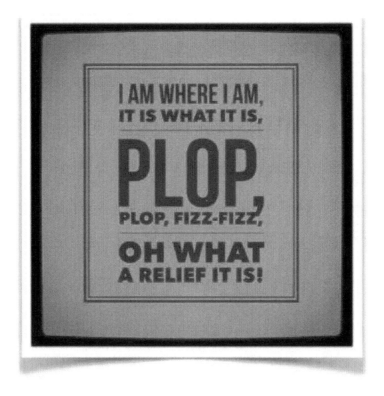

"It is what it is." Don't make it worse than it is! I can't believe how many people do this and don't even realize it!

Years ago, I was dating a girl who was living with me at the time. She got up in the morning to go to work only to discover her car had a flat tire. She came running into the house, yelling, "Oh no, I am going to be late! I can't be late!"

"I have a flat tire!" She gasped, adding that it wasn't safe for her to drive on wet roads, and it rained the night before, and before I knew it, she proclaimed, "I need four new tires, and I am going to get fired!" Then she said, "My car's transmission is getting worse, and it needs a paint job, and I don't know what I am going to do. I can't drive my car, I need a new car, and I am going to get fired!" It sounded as if her life was over and she was about to get struck down by lighting.

Do you see what happened? This is not a female thing, either. I have male clients who can take one wrong thing and turn it into Godzilla.

It's the art of exaggeration applied in a negative way! It's riding the Bitch Train and focusing on everything that is wrong instead of right! Due to the Law of Attraction, what you focus on expands, and a flat tire can easily turn into "I need a new car, and I am going to get fired and my life is over!!!!"

Okay, mistake #8 is learning to accept where you are in your life! You must start living in the NOW and enjoy the journey! Make the best of your situation. Remember, your situation can't get any better until you feel better about your situation. By doing this, you will be letting go of your resistance, getting yourself off the Bitch Train and onto the Bliss Train!!!

Here are 2 final reminders of things you can do that will help you make peace with where you are so this will no longer be a problem:

> **1.** Stop trying to FIX things from a place of feeling upset. You have to ACCEPT things in your life. Take responsibility for creating them, and then FIX your vibration by changing your thoughts and beliefs on the subject! If you want to create lasting change, then you must change your core vibration! How do you change your core vibration?

> **2.** The next time you find yourself frustrated and annoyed about your current situation, feeling that things are not getting better fast enough, jump up and say, "**I am where I am, it is what it is, plop, plop, fizz-fizz, oh what a relief it is!!!**" You might need to say it ten times and then deliberately focus on what is good, what is working in your life, by asking key questions that we already covered! Then find a way to make the best of things!!

Now that you know how to let go of all that resistance, I bet you feel one million pounds lighter! If you don't, just know that it takes practice and a determined desire to feel better. So start practicing and feeling better!

It's time to move onto the next biggest manifesting mistake that people make! This one mistake takes the FUN out of life faster than popping a hot air balloon!

BIG MANIFESTING MISTAKE #9

There's an old saying, "Don't take yourself too seriously because no one else does."

Have you ever taken yourself or life too seriously?

Ohhhh boy, do I know all about trying too hard and becoming serious! I used to have a serious problem! Watch my Toastmasters speech on YouTube called "R U 2 Serious?" at http://youtu.be/3HsCIu7ARKM

I have traveled the world from Amsterdam to Australia telling many stories, but the "Serious Problem Story" is the one where the most people come up to me afterward and say, "Thank you for sharing that story." WHY? Because they too have had or still have a serious problem. It's so easy to develop a serious problem, because in life we learn at a young age if we don't study hard, get good grades, get a degree, and get a good job, we will be failures.

When I was a kid, I was a goof-off. But I quickly learned that if I was going to become a success, I would have to become serious, stop wasting time, study and get smart.

Well guess what happened? I got too serious. And it worked for a while, as I became more successful. The more books I read and the more seminars I attended, the more success I attracted. But something happened along the way. I stopped having FUN. I started taking myself and my success so seriously!!! I no longer had time to just relax. First, I had to become super successful, and then I would have fun!

I had it all wrong! Life is supposed to be FUN! The most successful people in life are the ones having the most fun! They are doing what they love, and they are incredibly focused - but not serious!

We too can be focused without being serious. A gentlemen came up to me after one of my talks and said, "The word 'serious' is not allowed in my family!" WOW, this guy was serious. Just kidding!

I see this serious problem in so many people trying to get it right - read the right books, eat the right food, hire the right coach, etc. They're trying so hard to manifest the life of their dreams and change the world!

Underneath the desire to get it right is a FEAR of getting it WRONG! As I look back at my serious problem, I realize I was motivated by fear! If you have a serious problem, chances are good that you are also motivated by the fear of getting it wrong. Fear of looking stupid! Fear of wasting time or money! You want to get it right, and you want other people to get it right! If you are in management of other people, including kids, or have your own company, you know all about wanting other people to get it right!

But you do not want your motivation to be FEAR. You want it to be LOVE!

Having a serious problem is a sign that you are trying too hard - they go hand-in-hand! It says you are not trusting the Universe, you are not trusting yourself and you are not ALLOWING! That is one of the most important words you want to add to your vocabulary NOW and forever! ALLOWING is vital to your success!

Actually, according to Abraham-Hicks, there is a LAW OF ALLOWING! I believe it's as important as the Law of Attraction! We all know about the Law of Attraction - like attracts like, it's similar to gravity, it's always turned on and you can't turn it off. Blah, blah, blah.

The LAW of Allowing is where the magic happens!

Here's how, according to Abraham-Hicks, the creation process happens!

Step 1. You ask for what you want. Every time you know what you don't want, you automatically ask for what you do want, even if it's without words.

Step 2. The Universe says, "YES, I love you, it's done!" The second step is the Universe's job, not yours. It's none of your business. The Universe takes care of it for you.

Step 3. It's all about you ALLOWING your desires into your life! It's all about you activating the vibration that is the same frequency of your desire. Then you are on the same channel as your desire, and it can fall into your lap. It's feeling first, manifestation second.

Guess what, chicken butt! You can't ALLOW things to fall into your lap if you have a serious problem! That serious problem creates resistance, and that is the exact opposite of allowing.

Here's the deal: You have to get so good at feeling like you're already living your desire that you **don't care if it shows up!**

When you don't care if your desire shows up, then you know you have let go of all resistance! That can be a difficult vibration to hold, because reality beats you over the head, saying, "Look, you're still not there!"

It's learning how to detach from the outcome. Your desire is just an opportunity to focus and flow your creative positive energy. The real reason you want anything is because of how it will make you feel. It's not really about manifesting your desire. It's about the focus and flow of positive energy toward a desire!

So get so good at feeling it first on the inside that you don't care if it shows up on the outside, and then boom it will show up!

Many people ask what is that FEELING? Let's say they have never manifested a lot of money, so they say, "I don't know what having a lot of money feels like, so therefore I don't know how to feel it." That makes sense but guess what, the Universe gives you a lot of leeway. All you have to do is FEEL GOOD! You don't have to feel like a millionaire to attract millions of dollars. You don't have to feel like Romeo and Juliet to manifest your lover. You just have to feel good!!! That's how simple it is, and that's how to apply the LAW OF ALLOWING.

JUST FEEL GOOD NOW! Don't wait! Feel good now and dance and sing! For some of you serious people, that will take some effort! You have to deeply want to change, and you must really focus! Do not TRY to change - that is lame! Remember Yoda! "Do or do NOT. There is no try!!!"

I was finally able to let go of my serious problem and stop trying so hard when I heard Abraham-Hicks say to someone, "YOU CAN'T GET IT WRONG BECAUSE YOU WILL NEVER GET IT DONE!" I almost fell out of my chair!

WOW! That just blew me away! If we really believe we are eternal beings of light and love and that we have lived many lives, with many more to come, then it makes sense that it's impossible to get it wrong because we will never get it done! I believe it, and believing that makes me feel good! It makes me no longer fear getting anything wrong, because I know I will never get it done! There will always be the next desire and the next adventure!

Realize that when you're trying so hard to get it right, you're being driven by your fear of getting it wrong! It's because you hold the limiting belief that you are not doing enough or not good enough!

Say it with me: "YOU CAN'T GET IT WRONG BECAUSE YOU WILL NEVER GET IT DONE!" Start FEELING

GOOD right now! Start enjoying your life today! Accept where you are, and you'll start shining like a star. :-))))

Mistake #9 is trying too hard and taking yourself and life too seriously! Don't be serious, be focused. It's being FOCUSED that will ALLOW your success and happiness to manifest in your LIFE!!! Lighten up and have more fun. Don't take yourself so seriously because no one else is. Remember, life is a stage and we are all actors!!!

Here are 3 simple things you can do to drop your serious problem, (your resistance) and stop trying so hard:

1. Take two fingers and stick them in your nose and say, "I HAVE A SERIOUS PROBLEM!" Just kidding! Realize the more serious you become, the less success you will ultimately have. Be more playful in your everyday life. Watch more comedies and get around people who love to laugh. Take an improv comedy class, and I am serious about that. Okay, I am not serious, I am focused, but I do highly recommend you take an improv comedy class. This will get you out of your head, and you'll rediscover your playfulness and ability to laugh at yourself!

2. Start feeling good now for any reason you can find! FEELING GOOD is how you apply the LAW of ALLOWING to your life. It's Step 3 of the creation process,

and it's all you have to do. It's so EASY, it's STUPID!!!!! There are so many things you can FEEL good about right now, but you have to want to feel good! You have to focus on it and desire it before any desires show up! I KNOW I am repeating myself here a little because mistake #6 is all about feeling good, but repetition is the mother of skill! Go back and read #6 again, because feeling good is everything.

3. Stop operating out of FEAR! Know that you can't get it wrong because you'll never get it done! FEEL the relief. This brings you into the present moment! START operating from love, KNOWING that you are enough. LIVE IN THE NOW, and enjoy the journey. BOOYAH!

Now that you have let go of your serious problem and you're going to start ALLOWING things to happen instead of making them happen, your life is going to get so much easier. Things will truly start to fall into your LAP! Now let's move onto the next manifesting mistake that people make, #10.

Have you ever been stuck in limbo, not sure what to do with your life? Lost and confused? It's not a fun place to be, and I have been there more times then I care to admit! This next manifesting mistake is a biggie! When you do it, you're actually holding yourself in place, unable to move forward.

BIG MANIFESTING MISTAKE #10

We are living in exciting times, in times of extreme polar opposites. Life is so big, and it's easy to feel so small.

It's easy to forget that we are divine, sublime, cosmic, conscious creators. We have been brainwashed by society and ourselves into believing that what we see with our eyes is all there is to who we are. We believe in the illusions we are projecting.

WE FORGET that we are so much more then what we can see and touch!

The truth is we are more SPIRIT then we are physical.

We are more light and love than we will ever be dark and fearful!

We are Source in a physical body made up of positive VIBRATING energy! We are the creators of the Universe we live in! We are Divinity, God and Source Energy in physical manifestation!

You've probably noticed that a metaphor I like to use is that life is a movie and we are all actors. As an actor playing a character, you can rewrite the script if you don't like the movie you're in. Did you hear that? You, right now, can rewrite the script. By knowing the 13 Biggest Manifesting Mistakes and how to stop making them, you have nothing holding you back. You can create a new LIFE starting today.

Imagine that you're invited to a costume party, and you go all-out and spend $1,000 on a costume. Let's say you dress up like a pirate. You have your hair and makeup done by a professional, and everything about your look is authentic. You go to the party, and everyone is blown away with your costume and acting skills because you play the part super well. You've got the dialect down as well as the walk. You are the hit of the party, and everyone plays along with you. You are so good at it that you fall in love with the character.

You fall asleep that night wearing your costume and wake up the next morning believing that's who you really ARE!

At first everyone plays along, but after a week your real friends tell you, "Come on, stop being a pirate. This is not who you are."

In disbelief, you argue back with them, now even more determined to prove to yourself and everyone that you are a

PIRATE!! YOU continue being this fictional character for the REST of your LIFE! (I know that's extreme, but I'm making a point.)

NOW let's bring this metaphor home. Right now, you are a fictional character walking around believing this is who you are - your name, address, job title, age, weight and height. And guess what? YOU ARE RIGHT! You have created a brilliant character and everyone, including you, believes you. You should win an Oscar!

Underneath the character, you are actually a divine, sublime, cosmic, conscious creator. Unlimited by imagination and thought, you are an eternal being, and this life is a magical dream where it's IMPOSSIBLE to FAIL! **Did you hear that? It's impossible to FAIL!**

RIGHT NOW, START being Awesome, Amazing, Fun and Fantastic! Create a character in your mind and body TODAY that totally rocks. Then become that character and be the hero of your own story.

We are not here to suffer, or to pay our dues or to sing the blues. NO, NO, NO! We are here to ROCK and ROLL. We have already paid our toll, now is the time to take back control!

NOW LET'S TALK ABOUT HOW YOU CAN CREATE A NEW YOU!

The coolest thing about who you are is HOW you CREATE! It all starts with the thoughts you think! Your thoughts are made up of vibrating energy, and those thoughts go out into the world and attract back their equivalent to you! It is really simple! But yet we have made it SOOOOOO hard, myself included, because reality is so persistent and in-your-face.

Bottom line: You will start to vibrate and feel that which you focus on and think about consistently, and how you feel is how you attract.

So here's a key phrase to remember for the rest of your life:

FOCUS = FEELING!

What you FOCUS on you will FEEL! And how you feel is how you attract. This is not a cute quote in a book. This is LIFE CHANGING information that almost everyone overlooks.

One of the formulas I give in my workshops is:

It's called THINK. FOCUS. FEEL. ATTRACT! Most people experience the Law of NO Satisfaction because they don't get to the positive good feeling consistently! YOU have to THINK positively about what you want, then FOCUS on it until you start FEELING it, which means vibrating with your desire and then you will ATTRACT that desire.

THINK, FOCUS, FEEL, ATTRACT!

Now some people have mastered this formula... but in a negative way. They are great at thinking negative thoughts and focusing on what is wrong! They swear they are a positive person who reads all the positive thinking books, but underneath it all, they are feeling negative about many things!

This is a case of misdirected thought. They think and feel positive, but then they think and feel negative. They cancel themselves out and end up stuck in the middle!

Then they give their power away and say, "I don't create my reality! Something else must be going on - past life, sacred contract or evil entity!" NO, you just suck at thinking positive, feeling positive and staying positive! You let everything bother you and make a big deal about stupid stuff. STOP IT!

At one time, I did not see myself as an artist. I was good at art in high school, and I had a great art teacher, Mrs. Burwell, who recommended I go to art school. That seemed like a fantasy at first, but after high school graduation, I did go to art school. I was then surrounded by artists, and because of this, I saw myself as an artist and I became an artist. I walked like one, acted like one and drew like one. WOW! I changed my identity. Because I redefined how I saw myself, I thought different thoughts and created new beliefs about who I was and how I was going to show up in the world.

After art school, I moved to Orlando, Florida, and started working in the film and television industry. I became a PA, also known as a production assistant. I quickly had another identity shift, started thinking new thoughts, and I became a glorified PA, a/k/a/ a piss ant. I started acting the part and I rocked it. I was now someone different from before. WHY? I changed my thoughts about myself and how I was showing up in the world. I did that for a couple of years and then I started TUT (Totally Unique Thoughts) with my brother, Mike, and my Mom. By then, I was fast becoming yet another new character. What was it? An entrepreneur. I had again changed my focus and thoughts and beliefs about myself. Woo hoo!

Do you see how I have been different characters in my life? So have you. Underneath it all, you are still you. But who is YOU? Do you realize the you who thinks you are you is nothing but a set of beliefs that you hold about yourself - a set of beliefs that makes up your identity?

Change your beliefs about yourself and you change who you are.

STEP INTO YOUR POWER and OWN your awesomeness TODAY!

KNOW YOU are the creator of YOU.

Let me ask you a few questions.

- ## Who are you really?
- ## How do you want to show up in the world?

If you dropped your bogus stories and limiting beliefs, who would you become?

- ## Who is ready to emerge?

Think of yourself as an actor who is creating a new character - one that is more in alignment with your true passion and creative power.

Maybe you're ready to become the artist, the writer, the producer, the entrepreneur, the creator! Start BEING the person you want to BE and KNOW you are an unlimited, divine, sublime, cosmic, conscious creator!

I dare you to start BEING the person you want to BE today!

Write a description of some characteristics you'd like to have - maybe more confidence, clarity, fearlessness, joy, creativity, leadership, more friendly and relaxed. Make your list, and put it on your bathroom mirror. Then pick one word a day, and focus on that word! So right now, stop reading, pull out a piece of paper and make a list. Put it on your bathroom mirror and pick a word every day. Focus on the word, feel the word, become the word while you're standing in the bathroom. Take back control of your life and START being AWESOME, Amazing, Fun and Fantastic.

Okay, so mistake #10 is NOT KNOWING WHO YOU REALLY ARE! BUT now you know you're a pirate! Just kidding! You are a divine, sublime, cosmic, conscious creator!

Life is your stage, and you're a skilled ACTOR. It's time to start playing the lead role and being the star in your own movie!

BOOYAH!

BIG MANIFESTING MISTAKE #11

Have you ever said, "EVERYTHING HAPPENS FOR A REASON?" I bet you have, or at least you've heard it said.

Most of us scratch our heads and don't often know the reason for what just happened. It's not until years later that we might figure it out.

Here's what I believe: Everything that happens to you is because of Mercury going retrograde. Just kidding. Please don't give your power away to Mercury going retrograde. Mercury only has power over you if you give it power. I believe everything that's happening to you is because of the Law of Attraction.

That's it, mystery solved. You're welcome. :-)

Now I know some of you are going to disagree with me and say, **"Everything is not about Law of Attraction.** There are outside forces that affect us." OKAY, you do not have to agree with me. I just want you to be open-minded and consider what I have to say. I believe LOA operates clear to the far corners of the ever-expanding Universe and is always bringing things together that are vibrating on the same frequency. Like attracts LIKE!

I love the consistency and precision of the LOA. It is always giving YOU BACK exactly what you are vibrating out to the Universe! This is hard for a lot of people to deal with when things are showing up in their life that they DO NOT LIKE or want! They logically think there must be some outside force creating this or doing this to them, but the good news is THEY ARE DOING ALL OF IT! That's good news for all of us, because if we created the bad, we can create the good, the amazing and the beautiful!

The things that show up in your life that you do not want or like are telling you that you have misdirected focus and conflicting thoughts.

You have Lazy Lousy Focus Syndrome detailed in mistake #1.

Once you **take responsibility** for your thoughts and focus, knowing that everything is coming into your life due to the Law of Attraction, you can easily reverse anything that you don't like. You have the power – it is within you now!

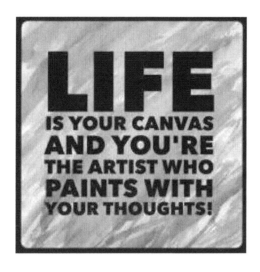

NOW let's say that you experienced an illness in your body or had a bad accident in your life. You might say, "NO WAY did I create this big problem!"

Not on purpose, of course NOT! (I am on your side - that's why I wrote this book.) But NO ONE else can think thoughts for you, no one else can paint on your canvas and no one else can write your story! We are all individual, independent creators, and you wanted it that way. You didn't want someone else creating your reality because they would get it wrong. Life is your canvas, and you're the artist who paints with your thoughts.

I have discovered that most people believe they create their own reality about 95-97% of the time. If you don't believe you create your own reality 100% of the time, then that means you believe there are victims, that the world is unsafe and you could be randomly hurt or killed on any given day. If you don't believe that you and LOA are 100% responsible for everything that is coming into your life, then who or what is??????

Santa Claus, the tooth fairy? (I'm being tongue-in-cheek.) If you don't believe LOA functions 100% of the time, then you must believe there is still something unknown operating in the Universe.

Maybe it's the dark side, evil spirits, Mercury going retrograde? What is it? I know many people suffer from Mercury going retrograde. I don't give Mercury and focus or belief, therefore Mercury does not cause havoc in my life. I truly believe there is only positive energy and love.

People will always have the choice to turn away from the positive energy through their mental focus, not allowing it to flow. Because of that, they can do some horrible things to themselves and others in a twisted effort to somehow feel better and reconnect with the energy.

You have heard it said that the moment you turn on the light, darkness disappears. I love Abraham-Hicks for saying there is no dark switch, there is no source of evil. Of course, many would disagree with me, saying, "History is filled with evil people and stories that would prove you wrong." But underneath the surface, LOA is always matching people up with precise, exact situations based on the vibration they are sending out to the Universe!

There are no accidents, and everybody is exactly where they "should" be, doing exactly what they "should" be doing according to their thoughts, beliefs and expectations. All of this creates the vibration of attraction they are sending out, and the LOA is responding perfectly every time!

Let me invite you to start believing that you do really create your own reality 100% of the time and that everything that is showing up in your life is due to the Law of Attraction. Can you feel the power within yourself when you start believing that you really do create your own life experience? And if you get honest with yourself and examine your past thoughts and beliefs, you will discover that everything that has shown up in your life has been a perfect vibrational match to your habits of thought. Now remember, on the surface you can think positive thoughts and say affirmations, but it's the feeling underneath that creates the vibration to which the Universe responds.

An example would be to say, <u>"I really, really want this thing I don't have."</u> <u>The vibration underneath that thought is, "I'm really, really aware that this thing I want in my life is missing!"</u> <u>The vibration you're sending out to the Universe is, "I am missing this thing, it's not here!" You feel incomplete without it, and it's that incomplete feeling that keeps you from attracting what you desire.</u>

BOTTOM LINE: Everything in the universe is vibrating energy. YOU are attracting everything into your life that is a vibrational match to your dominant vibration, courtesy of the LOA!

If you really want to take back control of your mind, body and soul, you have to KNOW that there is no escaping LOA. LOA dominates the Universe, and it's the reason behind everything. Please be open-minded and willing to look at your world with your LOA glasses on and see if things start making sense. Try on the belief that everything is vibrating energy and that LIKE ALWAYS attracts LIKE!

Okay, so mistake #11 is **FAILING TO UNDERSTAND THAT EVERYTHING THAT IS HAPPENING TO YOU IS**

BECAUSE OF YOUR MOTHER! Just kidding! It's the LOA. Period.

LOA DOMINATES THE UNIVERSE, AND IT'S THE REASON BEHIND EVERYTHING!

SOLUTION/FIX: For the next 30 days, take FULL responsibility for everything that is happening in your life. Don't look back and try to figure out all the stuff that went wrong in the past! WHY? Because all your power is NOW! The past has passed. Take FULL responsibility for everything that is happening in your life now. When you own it, you can change it!

Move forward today KNOWING that LOA is the reason behind everything that is showing up in your life. BECOME the example of possibility! LIVE the LOA! KNOW, KNOW, KNOW that you're creating your life experiences, and then you will start living happily ever after! BOOYAH!

BIG MANIFESTING MISTAKE #12

We all go through different phases in life when we care too much about what other people think. Doing this really messes up your positive vibration, and often times you sell yourself short.

"Care about what other people think and you will always be their prisoner." *~Lao Tzu*

Here is another great quote I found from Aaron Huey:

"The road to hell is paved with giving a crap what others think about you."

If you have ever given a crap what other people think, then you have been on the road to hell. You start micro-managing your every thought and action. You over-think everything because you're wondering, "What will they think if I say this, or wear this or do this? Will it get a positive response or a negative response?" You have to believe in yourself and make your own path.

Today most people are guilty of caring too much about what other people think. It has become an epidemic, even with those who say, "I don't care what other people think!" THEY do CARE! Otherwise they would not have to say it!

We care what our friends and neighbors think, as well as what our co-workers, potential lovers, and our families think! WE start changing our behavior to make other people happy, believing that if they are happy, then we can be happy too.

This is the start of the deadly vibration killer of **needing external validation** from other people so you can feel good. This is wiring yourself for pain, because you will NEVER be able to consistently make other people pleased with you and happy, no matter what you do! Let me say that again. <u>You will</u>

NEVER be able to consistently make other people pleased with you and happy, no matter what you do!

WHY? Because people change their minds and their values, and they are moody! When you stop being a people pleaser and just focus on making yourself happy, everything CHANGES! Do you realize that the greatest gift you can give someone is your own happiness? Being happy from the in

side out and being able to share that with anybody you want is a beautiful thing!

Trying to make other people happy can cost you your happiness because you stop being true to yourself by saying and doing things to please other people instead of you.

Here's a simple story that will help make the point! I was talking with a client who was somewhat annoyed, complaining that her boyfriend was not communicating enough with her. Sound familiar? She wanted to know, "What is he thinking and feeling?" She especially wanted feedback on how she was doing as his girlfriend. "TELL ME," she had pleaded with him. "I want to know! Give me feedback! Give me constructive criticism!"

I asked my client some questions and dug a little deeper. The reason she wanted FEEDBACK from her boyfriend was because she was a people pleaser and wanted to mold herself into the perfect girlfriend so that she would be loved and adored! WRONG. WRONG. WRONG! This is not how you want to show up in a relationship. She first needed to be true to herself. She first needed to love herself. There's nothing wrong with asking for feedback, but she was doing it without a foundation of love within herself.

She was trying to become the perfect girlfriend to make her guy happy! I asked her to focus on being her true self and operating from love and kindness in general and to stop worrying about what HE WAS THINKING! I encouraged her to start focusing on what she was thinking and doing and start BEING the best she could be while staying true to herself. I wanted her to make her happiness an inside job, her #1 priority, and then share that happiness.

Unfortunately, many women are raised to be good girls who quickly turn into PEOPLE PLEASERS! They often get a job where they are now being paid to make sure people are happy and getting great customer service or support.

All the while, people-pleasing women are living their life for someone else and playing by someone else's rules. This also happens to men. Meanwhile, both men and women who fall into this social conditioning are not following their dreams and doing what makes them happy first. They often build up resentment, get depressed and develop eating disorders or addictions.

People become addicted to external validation and have very little internal confidence to pursue their own dreams and not care what anybody else thinks.

So let me ask you, are you a people pleaser? Do you stand on your head to please other people? Do you seek external validation as a way to feel good and make yourself happy? It's an easy trap to fall into and can cause you lots of pain and needless suffering.

Of course, you don't think of it in terms of needing external validation. You see and feel it as a job well done. You feel pumped up from your good deed or services rendered or from being an awesome husband or wife. That IS awesome, and there's nothing wrong with receiving external validation such as compliments, praise and recognition. But a people pleaser operates from low self-esteem, and like so many of us, is actually their own worst enemy! They give themselves no internal validation and compliments, so they feel empty inside. The way they fill that void is to please other people, which would be OK if they weren't doing it for the wrong reasons. While putting everyone else's needs in front of their own needs, they are really craving the confidence to live their life and do their thing.

Here's a metaphor you have heard before but it's worth repeating. In life, you have to put on your oxygen mask first before you can help someone else with theirs. You have to love yourself before you can truly love another. And we all want to love and help others, for we all came here to teach, inspire and be an example of possibility to our family, friends and the world!

I compliment you for reading this, because it says you are putting on your oxygen mask first. You are learning and developing your self- worth and confidence! BOOYAH!

Here are 3 ways to break free from people pleasing and learn to give yourself internal validation.

This might sound too easy, but you just have to start doing it and let go of what other people think. It does not mean to become rude and inconsiderate.

1. To find a balance between being kind to other people and true to yourself, you must learn to set boundaries and start doing what is right for you. Start living your life. Setting boundaries might mean you have to start saying NO with a smile.

2. Start practicing internal validation and become your own best friend! Compliment and appreciate yourself for the daily small things you do! Develop a positive internal voice that validates and appreciates yourself!

3. Develop your connection and relationship with your Inner Spirit Guide by meditating. Set aside time every day to connect to the Divine Spirit within you!

AND here's a BONUS suggestion: Follow your heart. Better said, do what excites you! That excitement and energy is your Inner Spirit Guide giving you direction. By doing what excites you, you will find your dreams coming true much faster! And you will automatically develop the inner confidence to be your true self and live your life not caring what other people think!

So to wrap up #12, STOP worrying about what other people are going to think, say and do about you and your dreams. Get everyone else out of your head. Remember, you came to Planet Earth to experience time, space and the power of thought and imagination. You came for the thrill of the ride and to expand, learn and grow. **ALL of it is for the joy of it! For the joy of it, not the struggle of it or the pain of it. For the joy of it!**

Yes, it's wonderful to share with other people and give to others and make the world a better place, but in the end it's about the joy you created for yourself and then shared with others! If you have been living your life for others, today is the day you step up for yourself! Today is the day you stop caring what other people think. Can I get a namaste? Can I get a hell yeah?

WOW! That was the 12th biggest mistake that we can make, and it's an easy one to slip up on, but now you know what to do!

And now for the final manifesting mistake #13.... Drum roll please!

BIG MANIFESTING MISTAKE #13

Boom-Chicka-Boom, it's time to shake the room. It's big #13.

One of the concerns I've heard at every workshop I've done for the past five years is, "How do I deal with negative people?"

"Andy, I'm the positive one, but my partner, spouse, kids, family are so negative! What do I do?"

Negative people are everywhere, and sometimes you wake up next to one. Oh, no. Did you marry a Negative Vortex Vampire? Sounds like you might need a garlic divorce attorney.

(Bad joke.) What you need are some tools for dealing with negative people.

So, how do you stay positive when you're surrounded by negative people who are killing your positive vibe?

Secret weapon number 1: Don't resist their negativity! Let them be negative, allow them to be as they are. WHAT? I know that sounds like a crazy answer. But what you resist will persist. Your resistance to their negativity keeps it coming.

The ONLY reason you want them to stop being negative is so that YOU will feel better. **This is a recipe for PAIN** that you are actually inflicting on yourself! HOW? Because if in order for YOU to feel better, they have to change their behavior, you are at the mercy of their behavior. One day they act like you think they should and you feel good, but the next day they're negative and you feel bad. You have allowed someone else's behavior to control your vibration of attraction.

GIVE IT UP! You will never be able to get someone else to think and behave the way you want! NEVER, EVER - even if they LOVE you more than life itself and they promise to be just the way you want them to be! They are human and are always going to be motivated by their own self-interest! They will forget your preferences, they will have bad days, and they will say and do stupid things. If how YOU FEEL is determined by their behavior, you have wired yourself for pain and have no one to blame but yourself!

The solution is to focus on yourself! *Lead by example. Be the change you want to see in others. Start walking the talk! Stop asking other people to change so you can feel better and then instantly YOU WILL FEEL BETTER! Love and accept them as they are! If you can't love and accept them, then stay away from them!*

You have to be selfish enough to take care of yourself first because otherwise, you really don't have anything to give anyone else. I see this happen often, especially with women who give and give to others but have not given to themselves first, so they become resentful and depleted. This can easily lead to over-eating, over-sleeping, over-working, anger and depression, as mentioned in mistake #12.

If you attract negative vampires, it's just contrast. Do you remember that contrast is your best friend? SURF THE WAVES OF CONTRAST, dude. When you see what you don't like in the other person, two things happen. You gain clarity on what you do want, and desire is born for something NEW! Then YOU have to stay focused on what you want! Look for it and you will find it! Now that you no longer have a FOCUS problem, that will be easy-peasy lemon-squeaky.

Let's say your partner does not like an idea of yours, and it's an important idea to you. Because they are your partner/lover, you feel that they should like your idea and support you. Essentially you are resisting their negativity, and this resistance messes up your vibration. It hurts you because you are now upset and vibrating negatively, and how you feel is how you attract.

Other people can NOT prevent you from getting what you want. You're just using them as your excuse for not doing better. As soon as you focus on their negativity, you're not focused on where you're going, so you are now holding yourself back.

Your desire is between you and the Universe! What you need is alignment with your desire, which I teach you in my <u>Vibration Activation</u>™ audio program! <u>You don't need anyone else to believe in your desire. Just you!</u>

One of my clients experienced a lot of resistance because her husband didn't think it was a good idea for her to follow her heart and get a job. She was quiet and compliant, but her desires kept coming to the surface. She began to resist his resistance, trying to convince him. This of course made him more stubborn and her more determined.

My client couldn't move forward as long as she was resisting her husband's resistance. When I pointed out what she was doing, she realized she was the only one in her way! After some more coaching, she realized her husband was just mirroring back her lack of confidence and lack of belief in herself.

We did some Vibration Activation work, and as she increased her belief in herself, she started to feel she was good enough and worthy! Then she no longer needed his approval, and the resistance was gone. She manifested a great job and is now doing what she loves. **And** her husband now supports her 100%. WHY? Because she came into alignment, started to believe in herself, realizing that it wasn't really about him but about her!

Here's a second secret weapon: When it comes to dealing with negative people, FOCUS on their positive qualities!

Just find one positive quality and focus on it! During the tough times in my life, I had to have **roommates** to help pay my mortgage. A couple of roommates were a little annoying and negative at times, <u>but rather than try to change them, I changed how I saw them.</u> I would focus on two or three of the things I liked about them, and I was amazed at how they started showing up differently in my life. It was a miracle!

REALIZE anyone who is annoying to you is vibrating primarily on a different frequency from you BUT there has to be a part of you on their frequency. Otherwise you would not see their negativity and be affected by it! Both of you have some negative vibes going, and it's okay. It's just **contrast. Surf the waves of contrast!** It's an opportunity to shift your focus onto what you do want and look for the positive!

The reason another person is negative is because they more than likely don't like themselves, their job or their life in general. THEY might have become their own worst enemy. You want to have compassion and understanding and see them as an ANGEL on EARTH! Maybe they're a fallen angel, but hey, we all fall down sometimes.

Here's a third secret weapon: Don't take others' negativity personally. Remember, their negativity is not about you! Realize it's their own negative crap they're projecting onto you! Remind yourself that what they think of you has very little to do with you and everything to do with them!

We all want to help and provide solutions, especially if it's someone we love. But remember, you don't have to fix their LIFE, and they probably don't want you to even try. More than likely, they like their life just the way it is! Even though they complain, sometimes it's just their way of getting attention. Remember, you're not responsible for their unhappiness! But you are responsible for your HAPPINESS! The sooner you let go of trying to fix them, the better you will feel.

If you want to help another person, you have to do it from a positive, loving place. You can't help someone if you see them as broken. You must see the best in them, knowing they are simply caught up in their own drama, caught up in their illusion of lack and limitation and crying for help. You have to see their divinity, and don't let them bring you down. (Although, sometimes you have to look out for yourself and keep your distance!)

Secret Weapon #4: Ask negative people for the positive side of the story. Recently, I made a "Fortune Cookie Friday" video on how to deal with negative people. One of the suggestions I offered: The next time someone is complaining about life, let them finish and then ask them to now tell you something positive!

This, more often than not, will create an interesting look on their face. You might have to empathize with their negative story for a moment, and you might have to coax the positive out of them. Be playful as you ask for the positive aspects or ask them to identify the GIFT in their situation.

It's a simple request on your part, and the person will feel obligated to tell you something positive after being so negative, especially if you ask with curiosity and playfulness. For example you might say, "WOW! That's an amazing story. I don't blame you for being upset or angry! Now tell me something positive!" OR "What's the gift in this story?"

If they don't have anything positive to say, it's because they're on the Bitch Train, and they don't have access to any positive thoughts. Compliment them and give them a reputation to live up to, such as, "Oh, you're great at finding the bright side of things."

Sometimes if another person is extremely negative, it's better to leave them alone rather than try to evoke something positive from them, because they might not be able to find it. It depends on how angry or negative they are.

But if you make this a general habit, your negative friends will know if they call you up to bitch, they are also going to have to tell you the positive side of the story! Either they'll start finding the positive on their own or they'll find someone else to listen to their complaints.

What if you created an expectation with negative people that if they are going to complain to you, they also must tell you the positive, and if they don't have any positive, then they can't share the negative?

Final Reminder: STOP trying to control the outside world. IT does not work and will never work! What you want to do is say, "Thank you, CRAZY world, bad governments, politicians, evil corporations, dictators, negative vortex vampires, ex-husband/wife, barking dogs, annoying roommate or co-worker. The truth is you were just mirroring back to me my vibration! **You're my best teacher.** You helped me discover more, become more, and ultimately give more!"

Here's the best way to approach other people: <u>Love them</u> <u>because you love to love</u>, because you LOVE to feel love moving through you. Because being a LOVER is who you really are! Because you don't want to miss an opportunity to experience your LOVING self! Say to all of them, "I love that LOA brought us together. I am now more because of you. THANK YOU for being YOU! I LOVE YOU!"

Let's REVIEW! Mistake #13 is letting negative people destroy your positive vibes! Here are the four things you can start doing right now to CHANGE how you FEEL about negative people!

NUMBER 1: Don't resist their negativity because what you resist will persist. JUST Love and accept them as they are! If you can't love and accept them, then stay away from them! If you married them and can't accept them as they are, then leave. But guess what? You take you with you, and the next person you meet will probably have the same or similar negative qualities. YOU HAVE TO CHANGE your perceptions, and then everything will change for you!

NUMBER 2: Focus on their positive qualities! Do this every day until it becomes automatic.

NUMBER 3: Don't take things personally! Whatever they think or say about you is more about them then it is you! USE THIS CHILDHOOD SAYING. "Whatever you say bounces off of me and sticks to you!" Try it - it works.

NUMBER 4: Ask the negative people in your life to tell you something positive! This is a good way to test yourself to see if you can NOT get sucked into their drama but remain focused enough to ask them for the positive. Ahhhhh, grasshopper, you will become master if you can see the positive in all situations!!!!

Holy flying guacamole! There you have it - the 13 biggest mistakes of manifesting. WOW! I know that was a lot of content for you to process. Be sure to go back and re-read sections, make some notes, and most important, start applying the action steps in your life! It takes time to develop a new habit of thought and action, so be easy on yourself when you get off track AND HAVE FUN with all of this! Don't try too hard and DON'T get serious. Instead, get focused! Remember that CONTRAST is your best friend, and reality is your creation. In order to create anything, it's always FEELING FIRST, MANIFESTATION SECOND!

About The Author

Andy Dooley is a co-founder of TUT.COM and the creator of the ground-breaking process for manifesting called Vibration Activation™. 3 easy steps that take the mystery out of manifesting.

Andy is a law of attraction expert, Vibration Activation™ coach, spiritual comedian and artist. And he likes to run with scissors...naked.

Be sure to check out <u>AndyDooleyTV</u> on YouTube for FREE videos that will enlighten and inspire you :-)

If you're ready to master Andy's 3 step process or want to attend a LIVE Vibration Activation™ Workshop check out www.andydooley.com